PRAISES FOR

LIFE LESSONS FROM CENTRE COURT AT WIMBLEDON

"In this insightful book, Brad emphasizes the critical role parents play in teaching and shaping their children to be the best they can be. Full of real life stories and practical applications, *Life Lessons from Centre Court at Wimbledon* is a must-read for parents and children alike!"

—Sean Covey, international bestselling author
of *The 7 Habits of Highly Effective Teens*

"*Life Lessons from Centre Court at Wimbledon* is a great read! It is a book that incorporates the lessons learned from playing on the biggest stage in tennis into concepts that will help parents teach their children to become the best THEY can be on the field or court [or] in the classroom. I highly recommend it to both young and old!"

—LaVell Edwards, BYU head football coach 1972–2000

"As the father of seven beautiful children, I need all the help I can get in raising them the right way. They mean more to my wife and me than anything else. This book gave me great ideas that will help me be a better father today. I believe it will have the same power for you!"

—Chad Lewis, former BYU academic all-American
and three-time pro bowl tight end with the Philadelphia Eagles

BRAD PEARCE

PLAIN SIGHT PUBLISHING
AN IMPRINT OF CEDAR FORT, INC.
SPRINGVILLE, UTAH

ISBN 13: 978-1-4621-1609-6

Published by Plain Sight Publishing, an imprint of Cedar Fort, Inc.,
2373 W. 700 S., Springville, UT 84663
Distributed by Cedar Fort, Inc., www.cedarfort.com

LIBRARY OF CONGRESS CATALOGING-IN-PUBLICATION DATA
Pearce, Brad, 1966- author.
Life lessons from centre court at Wimbledon / Brad Pearce.
pages cm
ISBN 978-1-4621-1609-6 (alk. paper)
1. Pearce, Brad, 1966- 2. Tennis players--Biography. 3. Conduct of life. 4. Self-realization. 5. Wimbledon Championships (Wimbledon, London, England) I. Title.
GV994.P34 2015
796.342092--dc23
[B]
        2015003327

Cover design by Shawnda T. Craig and Angela Decker
Cover design © 2015 by Lyle Mortimer
Edited and typeset by Eileen Leavitt

Printed in the United States of America

10 9 8 7 6 5 4 3 2 1

Printed on acid-free paper

I would like to dedicate this book to my parents, Wayne and Carol Pearce; my siblings, Evan, Leslie, Robert, and Diana; Merrill and Linda Fisher; my wife, Cindi, and her parents, Charles and Oranee Abbott; our children, Jordan, Tara, John, Matthew, Joshua, and Halle; the late Harold Turley and his wife, Elaine; the many great friends, mentors, and coaches I've had through the years—and to all parents who are striving each day to teach and help their children to become the best THEY can be.

CONTENTS

CONTENTS

FOREWORD
BY LLOYD NEWELL

About a decade ago, on a cold winter night, I met Brad Pearce at the Brigham Young University indoor tennis courts. I was there playing tennis with my eleven-year-old son, McKay, who was showing great interest in tennis. We went to BYU to see if we could spend some time on the courts and improve his game. At that time, I could still teach him a few things about tennis, and he thought I was pretty good on the court. But I knew I was way over my head and needed help.

On one of the other courts was a man giving a lesson. Watching how confident and competent the man was, as well as how patient and encouraging, I wanted to get acquainted. Perhaps he could help McKay. I had no idea who he was.

When the man finished giving the tennis lesson, McKay and I went over and began asking him some questions, getting some pointers, and asking for advice. From that day forward, our family became dear friends with Brad Pearce and his family.

Brad has been a friend, a cheerleader, and a coach for every one of our children. All four of our children have attended his summer tennis camps; all four were given not just tips about tennis but also life lessons that we hope they will carry with them forever.

That is what this book is about. Brad uses tennis as a metaphor for life, as a means to discuss how and what it takes to become successful at life.

Life is about so much more than tennis, as Brad will be the first to tell you, but tennis provides a great way to talk about life.

Think about some of the terms of tennis: *service, love, game-set-match, advantage, fault, double fault*, and so on. In so many ways, life is like a tennis match. It provides countless ways to experience wins and losses, triumph and tragedy; and life presents for us countless opportunities to learn and grow, stretch, and become better.

Brad has experienced firsthand life lessons from Centre Court and from family life, and I am grateful and thrilled that we now have this book to learn from him.

Brad and his beloved wife, Cindi, have raised an impressive family whom we value as friends. We know each of their children well. They have each succeeded in their chosen fields of endeavor—excelling in sports, scholastics, and a range of extracurricular activities. They are devoted to their family and to their faith, acknowledging God in all they do. As you will learn in these pages, I know that their achievement comes from a family culture where talent, hard work, goal setting, determination, and striving for excellence resides in the walls of their home and in their hearts. As a family, they are exceptional in every way.

I have learned that every great effort is fueled by a compelling vision. Sculptors see potential in a stone, builders begin with the end in mind, students envision a future diploma, and parents see greatness in the most ordinary child. The biblical wisdom of centuries ago still rings true today, "Where there is no vision, the people perish" (Proverbs 29:18). With vision and diligence and the Lord's sustaining influence and divine help, we can succeed at life.

This valuable book provides an inspiring roadmap to assist individuals and families, parents and children, with helps and ideas along the journey of family life.

Lloyd D. Newell
February 2015

PREFACE

In 2012, I spoke at BYU's Education Week on the topic of "Lessons from Centre Court at Wimbledon: Teaching Your Children to Become the Best THEY Can Be." I put together a presentation with the major ideas and principles relevant to the topic that my wife, Cindi, and I had focused on in creating our family culture and raising our six children. I presented to a packed house in the room I was assigned, and I felt very encouraged that my concepts and ideas were well received. As I finished answering questions from some who had stayed after, I was approached by Angie Workman, an acquisitions editor from Cedar Fort Publishing. She said that she thought my concepts and ideas were "fresh, compelling, and relevant to parents," and asked if I would think about expanding on the themes and writing a book for parents to be published by them. This book represents the "expansion" of that original presentation.

This really isn't a sports book. But I have used my journey to Centre Court at Wimbledon and the lessons learned as a backdrop to the far more important topic of teaching our children (the next generation) to become the best THEY can be, recognizing that our children all come endowed with different aptitudes, talents, and interests. This book isn't about raising your children to become champions or the best. This book is, however, about helping your children to reach their own individual and unique potentials.

You might have noticed that I capitalized *THEY*. It's purposeful. Achievement is not comparative; it's individual. The "race," if you will, is not against anyone but ourselves; there are no winners and losers, even though the world tries to teach us different. It's about helping our children reach their potential, whatever that is. That's the goal—and it's individual. This book and each of the Life Lessons is intended to give you as a parent some ideas, thoughts, and concepts to help you teach your children to become the best THEY can be.

If you find something in this book, even just a sentence or two, that helps you toward that end with your child, then my purpose in writing this book will have been served. I wish you success in this most important work.

Brad Pearce
February, 2015

ACKNOWLEDGMENTS

I would like to thank Angie Workman, who first "recruited" me to Cedar Fort after hearing my BYU Education Week presentation in the fall of 2012; Steve Acevedo and Whitney Lindsley for keeping the project alive; my editor, Lynnae Allred, for being my sounding board and go-to person at Cedar Fort; Eileen Leavitt, my awesome copyeditor, for her meticulous attention to detail and design; Shawnda Craig and Angela Decker for their excellent cover design; the team of behind-the-scenes people at Cedar Fort; and finally, Lyle Mortimer, the founder of Cedar Fort Publishing, for making it all possible.

Special thanks and gratitude go to my wife, Cindi, who provided me with the encouragement to begin this project many years ago, her review of the final manuscript, and her support to see it through to the finish; my daughters, Jordan and Tara, who helped with the writing and editing; and members of my teams and the thousands of BYU campers I've been able to teach these principles to through the years.

And lastly, thanks to all of my children: Jordan, Tara, John, Matthew, Joshua, and Halle, who have made great choices in their lives and are striving to become the best THEY can be. I am blessed to be their father.

INTRODUCTION

I went to the same Earls Court Italian restaurant, *La Pappardella,* and ordered the same thing I had been eating for the past nine nights: caprese avocado salad and "pizza bread" followed by penne all'arrabbiata. I wanted to stick with what had brought me this far ("dance with the one who brought you") because tomorrow I would be playing the biggest match of my career against the number one player in the world, Ivan Lendl, in the quarterfinal round of Wimbledon.

Each win to this point was drawing me inexorably closer to my dream of winning Wimbledon, a dream I had held from the time I was six years old and watched Ken Rosewall and Rod Laver play in the finals of the 1972 World Championship Tennis (WCT) finals. I was taking one match at a time, never looking beyond the opponent right beside me in the draw. One thing that was definitely in my favor was that our match was scheduled for Court #2, known as the "Graveyard Court" because many a top seed had been "buried" (lost) there throughout the long history of Wimbledon. I had just beaten Australian Mark Woodforde quite handily in straight sets, 6–4, 6–4, 6–4 on that same court, so I was very comfortable in that setting. I had already begun visualizing the points that would be played between me and Lendl on that very court the next day.

I woke up to another drizzly morning in London, so I knew it would be a long day of "hurry up and wait"—that is, hurry over to the indoor courts to get a warm-up; eat a proper lunch perfectly timed with the start

1

of the match; and then spend most of the day waiting because of the rain delays, never really knowing if I was going to play until I was actually on the court. By late afternoon it had stopped raining, the sun was starting to poke through the clouds, and the covers were being taken off the courts. It looked as if we were going to play after all, which was good, because I was ready.

About halfway into my warm-up, an assistant referee had come over to my court and asked if he could have a quick word. He told me that there was a court change, and I would now be playing on Centre Court. This changed things dramatically. Now it was more than just a tennis match to be played on July 4, 1990; it was a match that would be viewed on worldwide television with the pomp and pageantry of playing on the most hallowed court in all of tennis—Centre Court at Wimbledon.

Down two sets to love, Lendl serving at 5–6, 30–40, I had a great opportunity to get back in the match. Lendl missed his first serve; here was my chance. I figured he would be coming into my backhand with his second. Before he hit his second serve, I had made up my mind that I was going to go for it and not hold back on my return. Sure enough, that's exactly what he did, and I was waiting for it. I stepped into the court and hit the exact shot I had envisioned for a clean winner. The third set was mine. The dynamic of the match changed with that backhand return winner.

As the match intensified, it became clear that we were both being driven by our goals: mine was to achieve my childhood dream of being a Wimbledon champion, and his was to secure the only grand slam that eluded him up to that point, and he desperately wanted it. To this day, I felt like I got a bad line call to get broken at 4–4 in the fourth, but there was nothing I could do about it. And even though I fought off one match point down 5–4, Lendl closed out the match on his second. The match was over; I had lost. My childhood dream of winning Wimbledon was not going to happen in 1990.

I retired from the Tour five years later in 1995 after a ten-year career. This match against Ivan Lendl, the number one player in the world at the time, on the biggest stage in tennis—Centre Court at Wimbledon— ended up being the highlight of my career, and even though I didn't realize my childhood dream, I had made my mark in the world of professional tennis, being referred to thereafter as the "Stormin' Mormon" and the "Provo Powerhouse."

The lessons learned in getting to Centre Court at Wimbledon, and the lessons learned since as a teacher to thousands of youth (including working alongside my wife in teaching our six children), has convinced me that our children becoming the best THEY can be is not merely a result of innate genius, talent, or chance but is the result of a concerted effort on the part of parents to provide opportunities, teach, train, guide, and hold our children accountable to their own individual goals—and, when needed, to step in to save them from themselves until they know better.

This book is dedicated to the idea that teaching our children to become the best THEY can be is the most important work we will ever do in our lifetimes. I sincerely hope there is something in *Life Lessons from Centre Court at Wimbledon* for you and your children. If so, then this book will have been a success. Teach your children to dream big dreams and go for it!

LIFE LESSON #1

ENCOURAGE YOUR CHILDREN TO DREAM BIG

"If you can dream it, you can do it."[1]

—Tom Fitzgerald, a Disney Imagineer

Teaching our children to become the best THEY can be starts with encouraging them to dream big. Whatever I have accomplished thus far in my life has stemmed from my parents, who taught me to dream big, set clearly defined goals, and then tirelessly and relentlessly work toward achieving them.

I was six years old in 1972, and I can vividly recall sitting in the family room of our home in Provo, Utah (we lived next to BYU football legend LaVell Edwards), watching Ken Rosewall and Rod Laver playing in the finals of the WCT finals in Dallas, Texas. This particular match has been called the match that made tennis in the United States and is widely recognized as one of the best tennis matches of all time. I can't speak for the other 21.3 million viewers, but I know that watching this match "lit my fire." I remember that Rod Laver wore a red shirt during this match, and even though he lost, it became my goal to play like him.

Since my father was the tennis coach at Brigham Young University, I had begun my tennis career early, and at age six, I had already played in several tournaments. After watching the Rosewall-Laver match, I insisted on having a red shirt so that I could be like the "Rocket." I always saved my Rod Laver shirt to wear in the finals. I even tried to switch hands and play with my left, trying to duplicate the exact way he hit the ball. That didn't work out so well, even though I still do a few things left-handed.

Children become inspired and motivated at young ages. To this day, I remember this match and the impact it had on me. I think it was at that moment that I decided I wanted to become a professional tennis player and win Wimbledon, what I perceived to be the biggest tournament and stage in tennis. It was about this time that Paul James, a legendary sports broadcaster for KSL radio in my home state of Utah, happened by the BYU tennis courts. He was a big tennis fan. I was already starting to show a lot of promise as a tennis player, which he noticed as he was watching me hit. As the story goes, he pulled me aside and asked me if I was going to play for my dad at BYU when I got older. My response was, "Heck no! I'm going to UCLA!" I had learned from being around my dad that UCLA was one of the few top tennis teams that he hadn't beaten to that point in his career as a tennis coach, and he had great respect for their coach, Glen Bassett. It's hard to say forty-three years later what exactly prompted me to blurt that out to him at that moment, but I did. My guess is that I had learned from my dad that UCLA had one of the best tennis programs in the country, and I instinctively wanted to play for the best. My dad never reprimanded me for my statement, even though he was BYU's coach. So I must have also felt validated by him that playing for UCLA was a worthy goal. Despite the fact that I was a very young, quiet, and shy kid, somehow I was not afraid of making outlandish statements like "I'm going to play for UCLA" or "I'm going to be a professional tennis player." It turned out that both dreams came true.

Dreams are becoming realities all around us every day. My parents started to cultivate this particular dream of mine from a very young age, which is something all parents can do. They simply followed my interest and provided opportunities for me to develop my abilities. In helping our children become the best they can be, it's important to notice what interests our children have, even when they are young. What do they like? What do they gravitate to? What interests and captivates them? Every child is unique in terms of their innate talents and abilities, but parents can do a lot to encourage a child, even if that child's goals seem out of reach or unrealistic.

My parents did all of the following to help make my childhood dream become a reality. They

1. Embraced my dream, showed interest, and affirmed my ambition.

2. Provided opportunities to develop my talent into actual skills.

3. Invested their resources in me (time, energy, and money).

4. Provided emotional support and positive feedback along the way.

5. Helped put together an action plan with a defined pathway to the end goal.

6. Moved from the role of alignment specialists to the passenger's seat at the appropriate time and then enjoyed the ride. (I'll speak about these terms in a different Life Lesson.)

I like Kevin Geary's suggestions on helping children turn their dreams into reality. He places an emphasis not on just the initial dream or achieving the dream, but rather on the process of achieving. He suggests five ways to help children turn their dreams into reality: don't deny their dreams, don't get in the way, set a good example, help them take action, and show support. I found the process of achieving to be most germane to this Life Lesson, because "it's about teaching children how to achieve anything. Achieving is a process of motivation, organization, intensity, and determination. We want them to learn the process so that even if their dreams change, their chances of success do not."[2]

Geary's use of the word *intensity* resonated with me because it was something I heard from my own father over and over again through the years. He believed that intensity was the key to success in any endeavor, be it in the classroom, on the court or field, or in the concert hall. My father must have hammered this into me before I was even consciously aware of it because to this day, my siblings tease me that I was the only six-year-old tennis player who had a fifteen-minute pre-match bench setup routine. I'd put on my Rod Laver red shirt and my match watch, then walk onto the court, put my match towel by the net post, take off my watch, place it next to my water bottle on the bench, and then get my racket out. Once everything was in its proper place, I was ready to play. My wife, Cindi, my children, and many BYU players I have coached through the years would be happy to share with you a few "legendary" anecdotes about this long-ingrained intensity, some admittedly more funny with the benefit of hindsight. Let's just say that I can relate to a statement made recently by Duke's Hall of Fame basketball coach, Mike Krzyzewski: "The thing that separated me as a coach is I have a real anger, passion, and emotion that I can get anytime."[3] That is me as well; it's all about intensity.

One of my favorite authors, Henry David Thoreau, wrote, "If one advances confidently in the direction of his dreams, and endeavors to live the life which he has imagined, he will meet with a success unexpected in common hours."[4]

Figuring out what our children's dreams and interests are is not a complicated thing. It's simply a matter of paying attention to what they enjoy doing, how they spend their time, what "lights them up," what they talk about, and what captivates them. It is up to us, as parents, to help our children advance confidently in the direction of their dreams. I had parents who helped me advance in the direction of my dreams, and because of that, I realized a lot more success than I otherwise would have. After recognizing what our children enjoy and are aspiring to achieve, the key is to provide opportunities for their interests, passions, or talents to more fully develop into actual knowledge and skills. These "fire-starters" don't have to be anything too spectacular—mine was a tennis match on TV and the purchase of a red shirt so I could be like Rod Laver. Of course, not all childhood dreams are going to become realities. There may be many fires that are started that don't end up becoming blazes, but I am grateful to my parents that they cultivated this dream and helped make it a reality for me. Do the same for your children. It would be very safe to say that accomplishment at whatever level by a teenager, or later in life as an adult, can be traced back to a parent, a coach, or some other trusted person in the life of that child that affirmed their dream or goal and said, "Go for it! You can do it! I believe in you!" Be that person.

NOTES

1. Tom Fitzgerald, Epcot theme park attraction *Horizons*, quoted in Dave Smith Disney Trivia from the Vault: Secrets Revealed and Questions Answered (New York: Disney Editions, 2012).

2. Kevin Geary, "5 Ways to Help Your Children Turn Their Dreams into Reality," Pick the Brain, last modified February 18, 2008, http://www.pickthebrain.com/blog/5-ways-to-help-your-children-turn-their-dreams-into-reality/.

3. Mike Krzyzewski, quoted in Jeff Benedict "The Education of Duke freshman phenom Jabari Parker," SportsIllustrated.com, last modified June 10, 2014, http://www.si.com/college-basketball/2014/02/19/jabari-parker.

4. Henry David Thoreau, *Walden* (New York: Thomas Y. Crowell & Co., 1910), 427.

TEACH YOUR CHILDREN
TO SET GOALS

"What you get by achieving your goals is not as
important as what you become by achieving your goals."

—Unknown

Teach your children to set goals. Goals need to be clearly defined, have time limits, and be worked toward—tirelessly and relentlessly.

As a result of my parents teaching me to set goals, today I am one of thirty-seven Americans since the era of "Open Tennis" (when the grand slams allowed professionals to play in 1968) to reach the singles quarter-finals of Wimbledon, making me a member of Wimbledon's Last 8 Club and giving me the nice perk of lifetime Centre Court tickets.

On September 30, 1984, I was the number one ranked junior tennis player in the United States and number five ranked junior in the world. Two years later, after completing my sophomore season at UCLA, I was a two-time all-American and headed to the pros immediately following the US Open in September. After representing the United States in international competitions in former Yugoslavia and France, I wanted to keep my amateur status to represent the United States one more time, this time behind the Iron Curtain of Soviet Russia at the Goodwill Games in Moscow. Returning home with gold and bronze medals, along with a memorable experience, provided a capstone to my amateur career. I was now a pro.

During my ten-year professional career (1986–1995), I had wins in singles and doubles against many of the greatest players to ever play the game. This list includes former number one players in the world and grand slam champions, including Pete Sampras, Ivan Lendl, John

McEnroe, Jim Courier, Boris Becker, Pat Cash, Stefan Edberg, Andrés Goméz, Goran Ivanišević, Michael Stich, Pat Rafter, Todd Woodbridge, Mark Woodforde, and many other notable players from around the world. I reached the finals of twenty-three professional tournaments (winning ten of them) and also reached the quarterfinals in doubles of both the Australian and US Opens. I was a traveling member of the 1990 Davis Cup Team that played in Prague and a member of the 1995 World Team Tennis Championship team—the New Jersey Stars. My wife and I, along with our oldest children (born while I was still playing professionally), had some incredible experiences as we visited thirty countries around the globe. In 1990, Cindi and I met with President Ronald Reagan and his wife Nancy. In 1995, I spent Ramadan in the palace of a Saudi Prince in Riyadh. I have friends from all over the world who have taught me to appreciate different cultures and religions. Just the other day, I signed my own Tour Star playing card sent to me by a fan from Germany. All of these cherished experiences and opportunities came about because my parents taught me to set goals and work hard to achieve them. And I had a lot of support along the way. Part of the purpose of this book is to share with you the process I had to follow in order to achieve my own goals. I am convinced that it is a formula that anyone can duplicate. It isn't easy, but it does work, and it starts with having a goal.

Your children don't need to be expert goal setters; they just need to have them written down and posted in a place that they will see multiple times during the course of their day. When I was a teenager, I used to have them on 3×5 cards stuck to the underside of the bunk bed above me so I could see them when I went to bed at night and when I woke up in the morning. I don't sleep in a bunk bed anymore (my wife said no), but I still keep my goals in a black journal that I keep by my side every day. These journals are a yearly log of my ideas and plans, and each one starts looking a little ragged by the time the pages are full and the journal is "retired" at the end of the year.

There is a wealth of information on goal setting that can be accessed with a quick Google search, but let me suggest that you start with something very simple. For example, we started our children setting simple goals in each of the basic areas of life: physical, mental, social, and spiritual. Keep in mind that the most important thing about goal setting is that you help your children find a system or method that is comfortable for them so it doesn't become an intimidating or overly onerous activity.

Once they're comfortable, they'll start getting more adept at it, and eventually they'll become what's referred to as a goal-oriented person.

Let me offer some suggestions on goal setting and an example. The first thing is to be specific in the outcome you are striving to achieve. It should be easily measurable and have a time limit. I'll share with you one of the major goals I set when I became a teenager: "I want to be the number one ranked eighteen-and-under junior player in the United States." This goal had an outcome that was a measurable (I will either reach the number one ranking or I won't) and it had a time limit (when I'm eighteen). This was a long-term goal, since it was set when I was around fourteen years of age. Then I sat down and wrote down all of the process goals that would go along with it, giving me a realistic chance of achieving that goal. My process goals were something like this:

1. Practice two to three hours every day except Sunday.

2. Condition and strength train six days a week.

3. Play at least two tournaments a month during the school year and a tournament a week during the summer.

4. Work on skill development during practice; practice deliberately.

5. Get plenty of sleep and eat well.

I relentlessly pursued the outcome, but on a daily, weekly, and monthly basis, I was focused on the processes that would lead to achieving that specific goal. In an academic setting, under the heading of "Mental," a person could set a goal to graduate from high school with a 4.0 GPA. This would be an *outcome goal*. The *process goals* to achieve that desirable outcome would look something like this:

1. Study two to three hours a day outside of the classroom.

2. Stay on top of homework, and don't get behind.

3. Study for tests well before the day they are to be taken.

4. Get help from teachers, parents, tutors, or peers when I don't understand something.

5. Don't ever "cut" class.

6. Be on time to class and sit in the front row.

7. Have everything prepared the night before important tests

(pencils, pens, scratch paper, review notes, snacks for energy, and so on).

8. Get a good night's sleep the night before tests, and don't get in a major sleep deficit.

9. Eat well, and drink plenty of fluids to stay healthy.

Hopefully the examples I've provided will help you, as a parent, get your children started setting the outcome goals they are motivated to pursue and process goals that they will be adhering to on a daily, weekly, and monthly basis to give themselves a realistic chance of achieving their desired outcomes.

SAMPLE GOALS

Physical: Do forty push-ups and sit-ups every morning and thirty minutes of cardio once a day; eat right; get required sleep at night

Mental: Do homework right after dinner and before bedtime; read for pleasure at least thirty minutes at night (when possible)

Social: Go on some sort of group date or activity at least once a month; participate in Church activities and school events; be involved in extracurricular activities

Spiritual: Say daily prayers and meditate; read at least one chapter out of the scriptures and other inspirational material every morning; attend seminary and Church meetings; perform service

Checking the Boxes

There's a term I like to use called *checking the boxes*. I explain what this means in my goal-setting seminars that I conduct during my summer tennis camps at BYU. Essentially, checking the boxes means that when you start the goal-setting process, you start with smaller goals first and move to bigger and bigger goals as you start putting check marks in the boxes along the way. It's just like putting a check mark next to a completed item on a task list. And let me tell you, there is nothing more satisfying or affirming than putting a check in a box of a goal that was accomplished. The power of this practice, or ritual, cannot be underestimated. To this day, I love putting checks in boxes of goals that were set and accomplished; it never gets old. Here is an example of the boxes that I "checked" on the pathway to Centre Court at Wimbledon:

Tennis Goals: Pathway to Winning Wimbledon

☑ Become the best player in my high school

☑ Become the best player in my city

☑ Become number one ranked player in the state of Utah

☑ Become number one ranked player in the Intermountain Region

☑ Become number one ranked player in the United States

☑ Become a top collegiate player

☑ Become a professional

☑ Win a professional event

☑ Get a high enough ranking to make the cut for Wimbledon (top one hundred)

☑ Make it to the second week of Wimbledon or better

☐ Win Wimbledon (Unfortunately, I was unable to put a check in this box.)

Teach your children to set outcome and process goals, to work tire-lessly and relentlessly to achieve them (while making adjustments), and to take pleasure in the sense of accomplishment and achievement they will feel as they start checking the boxes along the way. Get them started today!

TEACH YOUR CHILDREN TO WORK AND PRACTICE DELIBERATELY

"People don't understand that when I grew up, I was never the most talented. I was never the biggest. I was never the fastest. I certainly was never the strongest. The only thing I had was my work ethic, and that's been what has gotten me this far." [1]

—Tiger Woods

In teaching your children to become the best THEY can be, teach them to work and *practice deliberately*, a term that will be defined shortly. As far as I'm concerned, there is no substitute for work ethic in any endeavor. I can echo what Tiger said by admitting that I was never the most talented player. It's interesting to hear what a few famous people (who most of us consider to be geniuses today) said about the source of their so-called genius. Johann Sebastian Bach, in explaining away his achievements, said about himself, "I was made to work. If you are equally industrious, you will be equally successful." [2] Michelangelo's opinion of himself was similar to Bach's. "If people only knew how hard I work to gain mastery, it wouldn't seem [referring to his artistry] so wonderful at all." [3] I'm certainly not comparing myself to Bach or Michelangelo (perhaps Federer can be put in that category), but I did put in a lot hard work and thousands of hours of practice. And even what I just called "practice" isn't a precise enough definition anymore, as author Geoff Colvin points out in an article he wrote in *TIME Secrets of Genius: Discovering the Nature of Brilliance.* In fact, he writes, researchers today are redefining what the terms *genius* or *expertise* really mean by calling them "reproducible expert performance,"

15

which is further explained as "world-class achievement that isn't the product of randomness."[4]

He adds further to the discussion on work ethic and deliberate practice that I've addressed in this lesson by sharing some additional light on the nature of brilliance: "So brilliance doesn't spring from any of the obvious sources. Where, then, does it come from? It is rooted in what researchers led by K. Anders Ericcson of Florida State University call deliberate practice. And although it does involve lots of hard work—thousands and thousands of hours over many years—deliberate practice is something very different from what the rest of us might think of as practice."[5] He then goes on to explain how "deliberate practice" is different than garden-variety, old-fashioned "practice" when he says, "Deliberate practice has four main components:

1. It makes you better at the skills you need at a particular stage of development.

2. It pushes just beyond current abilities.

3. It is repeated at high volume.

4. It provides continuous feedback."

He adds, "At an hour a shot, genius-making is one long slog. Recently the number that has been riding the pop-culture wind is 10,000: the hours it takes to become special in any given discipline. That figure first turned up in a landmark study of violinists by Ericsson and his colleagues, and it has since been reinforced in many others. But often, discussions of that finding overlook a most important detail: that 10,000 hours isn't of work in general, but rather of deliberate practice. . . . In the end, we're talking about it taking at least 10 years to unleash genius, 10 years of reaching for what can't quite be attained, of making mistakes, of suffering failure. Ericsson minced no words when he said it's 'not inherently enjoyable.'"[6]

If you want your children to get on the pathway to becoming the best THEY can be, get them in whatever way you can—helping, teaching, training, guiding, motivating, inspiring—to start logging their hours of work and deliberate practice today.

In my current role as a collegiate tennis coach, I'm often asked what I look for in players that I recruit. My complete response is that I look for a combination of overall athleticism (talent), work ethic, skill, and mental toughness. Admittedly, early-on in my coaching career, I tended to be more attracted to players that I assessed to have great talent; they just looked better when they played. Through the years, though, I have been burned by talent too many times because talent does not always translate to success on the court. So now, provided the talent level is good enough, I look for work ethic and mental toughness. I like how NBA player Kevin Durant's mentor Taras Brown put it when he said, "Hard work beats talent when talent doesn't work hard."[7]

The ideal, of course, is the combination of talent, skill, and work ethic, but there are relatively few players that seem to have all three. Those that do, combined with mental toughness, are the ones we read about in the newspapers who are garnering the scholarship awards in academics, athletics, and the arts. Perhaps it's no coincidence that the individuals we often label as talented often have great work ethic too.

One of my favorite books, *Outliers* by Malcolm Gladwell, explains and illustrates this principle perfectly, and Julie Mack, a columnist for the *Kalamazoo Gazette*, summarized Gladwell's comparison of talent versus work ethic this way:

> I know a woman who used to live in a townhouse next to Derek Jeter and his family. Jeter was a young boy at the time, and my friend recalls that Jeter would entertain himself by throwing a baseball over the townhouse roof. He'd then run to the other side of the building in time to catch the ball. Jeter would play this game for hours, she said. My friend laughingly recalls that she found it a huge irritation because the ball would often bounce off the roof, waking her baby. For me, the point of the story is that Jeter's considerable abilities didn't happen by chance. He became a baseball star because he worked it, all the time. In fact, others who knew Jeter in his Kalamazoo days have similar stories about how he was continually practicing his baseball skills.

Mack emphasizes Gladwell's observation that Jeter's success wasn't due to his exceptional talent but was due to his exceptional work ethic, and successful people are typically the hardest and most dedicated workers. Her essay continues:

> Examples aren't hard to find. From Jeter to Michael Jordan to Tiger Woods, superstar athletes say the key to their success has been their work ethic. Author Truman Capote used to advise would-be authors to write as much as possible every day. Even hedonistic rock stars such as Keith Richards and Eddie Van Halen have talked about

how, when they were younger, they would lock themselves away for days on end to concentrate on making music. It's a useful model to consider when thinking about school success. . . .

Even beyond good grades, there's another reason for parents to cultivate a strong work ethic in their children. As students grow up and enter the job market, "soft skills" such as work ethic, persistence, and ability to follow directions and meet deadlines are highly prized by employers and rank as even more important than content knowledge. In the work world, being a hard worker is far more valued than being smart.[8]

Gladwell's research on this subject is remarkable and important. It emphasizes the difference between the "outliers" and the rest of us: "Once a musician has enough ability to get into a top music school, the thing that distinguishes one performer from another is how hard he or she works. That's it. And what's more, the people at the very top don't work just harder or even much harder than everyone else. They work much, much harder."[9]

I never really thought about whether I was talented or not, nor did my parents really dwell much on that topic. I simply was what I was as an athlete. I set goals according to my interests and desires and worked hard to achieve them, and I received a lot of help along the way. In a later Life Lesson, I'll talk about my defining moment, which I think best illustrates how commitment, dedication, and sacrifice (not talent) helped me to achieve what I did in the world of tennis. Keep in mind that there have been only three men to quarterback their teams to four Super Bowl wins in the NFL. Two of those three, Tom Brady and Joe Montana, weren't even selected in the first round of the NFL draft. In fact, Tom Brady of the New England Patriots was drafted in the sixth round and Joe Montana of the San Francisco 49ers in the third round. The talent experts in the NFL didn't expect anything exceptional from either of these now-superstars.

As such, we haven't spent a minute concerning ourselves with our children's IQs or other assessments of their innate talent or abilities. Instead, we've focused on helping them to set goals in accordance with our family values and their interests, and we've taught them to work tirelessly and relentlessly to achieve them. One of my all-time favorite fictional characters is Forrest Gump, played by the Academy Award–winning actor Tom Hanks. Even though Forrest was considered slow in thinking and not the least bit talented, he seemed to always be making the right decisions and doing the right things at the right times to have a life of achievement. Talent is overrated. In teaching your children to become the best THEY can be, teach them that talent is great but that work ethic reigns supreme in the classroom, on the court, or in the concert hall. Don't wait. The sooner you can teach your children that work ethic is far important than innate talent or intelligence, the sooner you can get them out logging their ten thousand hours of deliberate practice in the area they want to achieve big things.

NOTES

1. Tiger Woods, interview by Chief Roger O. Crockett at the W Hotel in New York, quoted in "The Business of Tiger Woods is Good," *Business-week*, last modified September 30, 2008, http://www.bloomberg.com/bw/stories/2008-09-30/the-business-of-tiger-woods-is-good.

2. Johann Sebastian Bach, quoted in Geoff Colvin, "The Long Hard Road," *TIME Secrets of Genius: Discovering the Nature of Brilliance* (NY: Time Home Entertainment, 2013), 94.

3. Michelangelo di Lodovico Buonarroti Simoni, quoted in Geoff Colvin, "The Long Hard Road," *TIME Secrets of Genius: Discovering the Nature of Brilliance* (New York: Time Home Entertainment, 2013), 94.

4. Geoff Colvin, "The Long Hard Road," *TIME Secrets of Genius: Discovering the Nature of Brilliance* (New York: Time Home Entertainment, 2013), 94.

5. Ibid., 96.

6. Ibid., 97.

7. "Kevin Durant Player Page," NBA.com, accessed March 6, 2015, http://www.nba.com/thunder/team/kevin_durant.html.

8. Julie Mack, "Derek Jeter is Pure Example: Hard Work is Key to Success in School—or Any Field," November 23, 2010, accessed March 6, 2015, http://www.mlive.com/opinion/kalamazoo/index.ssf/2010/11/hard_work_is_key_to_success_in.html.

9. Malcolm Gladwell, *Outliers: The Story of Success* (New York: Little, Brown and Company, 2008).

HELP YOUR CHILDREN DISCOVER AND DEVELOP THEIR UNIQUE TALENTS

"When it comes to developing character strength, inner security and unique personal and interpersonal talents and skills in a child, no institution can or ever will compare with, or effectively substitute for, the home's potential for positive influence."[1]

—Stephen R. Covey

While talent isn't everything, I am grateful to my parents for recognizing my unique talents and giving me opportunities to develop them into real skills. By age four, I could hit tennis balls back and forth with my dad, who observed that my hand-eye coordination and balance were unusually good for someone my age. Because my parents spent a lot of time around tennis players, they also noticed that I had a good disposition for tennis. I had the ability to concentrate and focus for an extended period of time and maintain emotional equilibrium—an even keel. They also discovered that I had possession of the three Cs—I was cool, calm, and collected under pressure.

Naturally, it made sense to get a tennis racket in my hand at an early age. However, they didn't have tennis rackets in 1970 for four-year-olds like they do today, so my dad had the handle of a squash racket cut halfway off and re-gripped. Voila! I had the first mini tennis racket for kids. He then got me started with the fundamentals of tennis, with an emphasis on *fun*. Of course, that doesn't mean that I didn't participate in other sports. I loved all sports, and my parents recognized that my activity in other athletic endeavors helped foster my athleticism in general. They supported me in playing Little League baseball, basketball, and skiing, but they never let me lose sight that I had a particular aptitude for tennis.

Elder Bruce R. McConkie, who served as a General Authority for the Church of Jesus Christ of Latter-day Saints, believed (as do all members of the Church) that all of us lived in a premortal life where we had the opportunity to begin to develop our talents. McConkie wrote,

> All the spirits of men, while yet in the Eternal Presence, developed aptitudes, talents, capacities, and abilities of every sort, kind, and degree. During the long expanse of life which then was, an infinite variety of talents and abilities came into being. As the ages rolled, no two spirits remained alike. Mozart became a musician; Einstein centered his interest in mathematics; Michelangelo turned his attention to painting. . . . Abraham and Moses and all of the prophets sought and obtained the talent for spirituality. . . .
>
> When we pass from preexistence to mortality, we bring with us the traits and talents there developed. True, we forget what went before because we are here being tested, but the capacities and abilities that then were ours are yet resident within us. Mozart is still a musician; Einstein retains his mathematical abilities; Michelangelo his artistic talent; Abraham, Moses, and the prophets their spiritual talents and abilities. . . . And all men with their infinitely varied talents and personalities pick up the course of progression where they left it off when they left the heavenly realms.[2]

All children are born with their own unique and varied talents. It then becomes our responsibility, as their parents, to help them discover and develop these gifts. Not only did my parents foster my unique talents, but they made a lot of sacrifices to give me opportunities to develop the necessary skills and competitive experiences to further my career as a tennis player.

When giving seminars to parents who want to help their sons and daughters excel athletically and academically, one concern I hear parents voice frequently is that their children don't have much interest in anything. It's a common concern, and I usually respond that fostering interests and unique talents is a process of discovery. It begins with exposure. If you've exhausted the soccer field, model-rockets, musical instruments, and at-home art projects, then maybe the next stop is the local museum, zoo, or planetarium. This doesn't mean you have to spend a lot of money (or really any money). Work within your budget. In fact, the story of Ben

Carson illustrates this idea perfectly. His life was changed with a Detroit Public Library card and a mother who devised a plan to give her sons the chance to reach their potential. With only a third-grade education, this hardworking mother made an astute observation: successful people seem to have a lot of books around, and they don't spend much time watching TV. She came up with a plan for her sons:

> Since she worked long hours, Mrs. Carson often didn't return home until the boys were in bed. Two days after the report cards arrived home, she left work early to check on her boys. There they were, as she expected, lounging in front of the TV. "Boys, you spend too much time in front of that television. You do not get an education from staring at television all the time. . . . From now on, you will not watch television, except for two pre-selected programs a week. . . .
>
> "And that›s not all," Mrs. Carson said. "In addition to doing your homework, you have to read two books from the library each week. Every single week. And when you're finished reading them, you must write me a book report just like you do at school."[3]

Bennie and Curtis, with the help of a friendly library staff, became avid readers. Ben's particular interest was rocks, and he'd hunt for interesting specimens along the railroad tracks in his neighborhood. One day, his science teacher held up a shiny black rock and asked the class if anyone knew anything about it. Ben startled the class and the teacher (and probably himself) by raising his hand to give the correct answer: "Obsidian."

This was a turning point for Ben. By the time he reached the sixth grade, he was at the top of his class. Today, he is a world-renowned neurosurgeon. He said: "Between the covers of those books I could go anywhere, I could be anybody, I could do anything."[4] Let's not forget that his achievements all came about from a mother who came up with a simple plan. I'm sure that Ben's accomplishments were even surprising to her. As parents, we don't really know what our children are capable of achieving, but that doesn't matter. All that matters is that we do our best to come up with a plan for them and try our hardest to foster their interests.

At the same time that you're discovering what interests your children might have, reflect on what resources or situations you and your spouse can use to your advantage in helping support their endeavors. For example, tennis resources were readily available for our family. Instead of paying a coach, I could teach them myself, and I found the time in the early morning hours before my work day started and before their school day started, which took some sacrifice on all of our parts. Figure out where you, as parents, can capitalize best within your own knowledge, resources, and experience to help your children.

As parents, we've tried to stand back and objectively see where our children "shine," what they seem to be good at, what they don't seem to be good at, and what they're interested in. It's okay if they're not good at everything; it's even okay if they are horrible at some things. Don't be so afraid that they might fail that you don't let them take risks. And don't be afraid to let them pursue interests that you wouldn't necessarily see as their niche or forte. Kids sometimes surprise you. We learned these two very important principles with our daughter, Tara. The first example is when she came home one day after school and declared that she was going to run for student-body president at Timpview High School. Keep in mind that she wasn't asking us what we thought, she was telling us what she was going to do. We asked a couple of questions, including who she would be running against. After getting all the information we needed, Cindi and I were thinking the same things (she's well-liked but was running against a boy who was very popular, and Timpview's history of electing females to the office of student-body president was almost nonexistent at that time), so we both immediately started trying to talk her out of it, suggesting other offices to run for that she might have a better chance of winning. This was all because we didn't want to see her fail, which we thought at the time was a possibility. To her credit, she listened to all of our concerns and simply said, "Well, I'm doing it. Are you going to help me win or not?" What do you say to that? We could only ask her what we could do to help. We rolled up our sleeves and went to work. At this point, the winning or losing was immaterial to the process of dreaming big dreams, setting big goals, and her willingness to do whatever she could to make it happen—the principle of *alignment*. Tara actually ended up winning the election. It was such a powerful learning lesson for Cindi and me on the concept of letting children take risks even though they might fail. They can often surprise us (as much as we think we know their capabilities).

Another story involving Tara illustrates the other point I want to make about not being afraid to let your children pursue interests when you don't think they have any talent or that "it's just not their niche or forte."

If you had read, as we did, some of the essays and stories she brought home from kindergarten through grade ten, you would have been painfully aware of our daughter's lack of literary prowess. Taking a line from *A Series of Unfortunate Events*, Cindi and I would say to each other that Tara must have been "speaking monkey," because we could not, for the life of us, find any meaning from the words she had strung together. Her writing was really that bad. When we tease her about it now, she says that what kept her at it and interested was her love of reading. She recognized that in order to excel in her dream job of teaching literature, she would also have to be able to write. So she worked at it and worked at it. As her parents, we thought she had zero, and I mean *zero*, talent in this area. We absolutely knew that this was not her niche or forte, but it was what interested her and kept her busy, so despite our misgivings, we supported and encouraged her because those were her goals—to become an accomplished and inspiring English teacher and successful writer.

To make a long story short, Tara was an English Sterling Scholar and was recently published in the *Utah English Journal.* She is currently teaching English at our local junior high, and she will graduate from BYU with high honors in an English teaching degree. She was also recently accepted into a master's program at Cambridge University—one of the most prestigious universities in the world to attend for her area of study. At the same time, she went through a very grueling interview process as a candidate for Teach for America, which she ultimately accepted. She will start her teaching this fall in the inner city of Boston while working toward a master's degree in education at Boston University. We couldn't be more proud of her for working so hard and overcoming so much to earn a place at Cambridge, but then ultimately turning it down to make a difference among those who, she says, "Need to be taught about following dreams and believing in themselves." What Tara accomplished is beyond what we thought she was capable of as a child. It has been a profound lesson for Cindi and me to learn that determination and persistence can take someone a very long way indeed.

As parents, we know better than anyone what our children's strengths and weaknesses are. We should try to help them build up their strengths and not to shelter them from their weaknesses. As legendary UCLA coach John Wooden put it, "Do not let what you cannot do interfere with what you can do."[5] Our kids knew that they weren't any less loved if they failed at something. We tried to use the dinner table as a safe place where successes and failures could be discussed—where we learned to laugh at ourselves—and so it became ingrained as part of our family culture that not everyone had to be good at everything. And that is okay. As a result, our kids never felt the need to hide weaknesses. As a family, we always get a good laugh out of the scene from *A Knight's Tale* when Count Adhemar says to William, "You have been weighed, you have been measured, and you have been found wanting."[6] Adhemar is quoted often in our home when someone has fallen just a bit short at something. Our children knew they might be teased by their parents or their siblings when they had a less-than-heroic moment (which we refer to as "a clown act"), but they also knew we'd be there to support them, cheer them on, and celebrate the successes along the way.

My mother had a philosophy that if you can excel in just one thing and become really good at something—anything—that that experience and process will eventually carry over into other things. Essentially, it's the age-old idea that success breeds success. She knew each of her children's strengths and weaknesses, so she saw to it that we all developed something that we were good at, believing that there would be a carryover effect.

One day, I happened to watch a cup stacking championship on TV. While I was impressed with how fast the participants could stack cups, I thought to myself, *What use will that skill be? What a waste of time!* Then I remembered what my mom believed and had to change my thinking to, *Good for them, they've become great at something.* Down the road they will transfer the concentration, discipline, and focus it took to become that good at stacking cups to other important areas in their lives. Who are we to say that this talent won't transfer to helping one of them become a great student or a successful professional? They have learned the principles of success: dream big, feed talent, work hard, practice deliberately, focus, and be persistent.

Cindi and I haven't lost any sleep from concern about the things our children haven't been good at. Instead we've "doubled-down" in those areas where we have thought our children could really make a difference and could set themselves apart. We relied on the idea that success, expertise, or excellence in just one thing will eventually lead to success in many other areas. Once our children understand how they've been blessed with talents unique to them and have learned the principles of success, the world becomes their oyster.

In teaching and helping your children to become the best THEY can be, don't spend a minute worrying about what they're not good at. Resist the temptation to protect them from failing or steering them away from something they like but may not be good at yet, because you never know. Instead, identify those areas where they have some unique talent or interest, and then encourage them to go for it. In other words, focus on those things they're naturally good at and have the right disposition for, and then put your resources into giving them the opportunities and experience that will lead to success in that area and long-term success in other important endeavors down the road. Teach your children that their talents come from God, but it is up to them to develop these talents for the benefit of others. As Hall-of-Famer Larry Bird said, "A winner is someone who recognizes his God-given talents, works his tail off to develop them into skills, and uses these skills to accomplish his goals."[7] That is the process my parents followed after they put that first sawed-off squash racket into my four-year-old hand.

NOTES

1. Stephen R. Covey, "Our Children and the Crisis in Education," *Huffington Post*, June 20, 2010, last modified November 11, 2011, http://www.huffingtonpost.com/stephen-r-covey/our-children-and-the-cris_b_545034.html.

2. Bruce R. McConkie, *The Mortal Messiah*, vol. 1 (Salt Lake City, UT: Deseret Book, 1979), 25.

3. Al Siebert, "From Poverty to Prosperity: The Story of Benjamin Carson, MD," Al Siebert Resiliency Center, accessed March 6, 2015, http://resiliencycenter.com/from-poverty-to-prosperity/.

4. Ben Carson, *One Nation: What We Can All Do to Save America's Future* (New York: Sentinel, 2014).

5. John Wooden, quoted in "The Wizard's Wisdom: 'Woodenisms,'" ESPN.com, June 4, 2010, http://sports.espn.go.com/ncb/news/story?id=5249709.

6. *A Knight's Tale*, directed by Brian Helgeland (Culver City, CA: Columbia Pictures, 2001).

7. Larry Bird, quoted in Ryan Frischmann *A Skills-Based Approach to Developing a Career* (Bloomington, IN: Trafford, 2013).

THE PRINCIPLE OF ALIGNMENT

"Nothing can stop the man with the right mental attitude from achieving his goal; nothing on earth can help the man with the wrong mental attitude."

—Unknown

Over the years, I've taught thousands of teenagers in goal-setting seminars at my BYU tennis camps, helping them to dream big. I show them a brief clip of my quarterfinal match against Ivan Lendl and tell them that my dream from when I was very young was to become a professional tennis player and win Wimbledon. They see me give an emphatic fist pump as I hit a backhand return to win the third set. They look at me, the guy standing in front of them, and question whether that's really me that they're watching, actually playing on Centre Court, because up to that point they have solely looked at me as BYU's head men's tennis coach and the camp director. And they always comment on my shorts, wondering if they are actually shorter than former NBA great John Stockton's.

We then go around the room and have them introduce themselves and tell us where they are from and what their goals are in tennis. I explain that what I am about to teach them applies to any goals they may have in any area of their lives (academic, athletic, musical, artistic, and so on), but since they are here to improve their tennis, we're going to discuss their tennis goals. There is a reason I have them go through this process. I want them to vocalize their goal in front of their peers so they take ownership of that goal. I have found that when we make our goals public, we become more accountable to them. I also make it clear that I want them to express what's truly important to them: "Don't give me a line or try to guess what you think I want to hear. Sincerely and without equivocation, tell me what you're trying to accomplish in tennis and why you're here. What is *your* goal?"

Some express very ambitious goals, and some express that they just want to learn to enjoy the game and have fun or beat a family member. For the dads out there, your kids often want to beat you more than they want to beat anyone else in the family, so consider yourselves warned. Your kids are coming after that alpha position on the family tennis ladder. (As an aside to dads, my father likes to joke that he used to be number one in the state, but now he's not even top ten in the family. I fear that my day is coming as well, but trust me when I say I'm holding on with a kung-fu grip.)

Something I really enjoy about the teaching and coaching process is getting my students and players to be introspective and to really understand their own internal motivations for what they're doing—the goals they set and how they spend their time.

After everyone has stated their goal, I teach them to dream big and set goals in those things that are important to them in each category of their life. I state that it's relatively easy to set goals ("I want to be an astronaut," "I want to be a fighter pilot," "I want to play in the NBA," "I want to win Wimbledon," and so on), but the hard part comes with actually doing the day-to-day, week-to-week work that will give them a realistic chance of achieving the stated goal. I call this the *principle of alignment*. I believe it's a principle because it's a "fundamental truth that may be used in deciding conduct or choice."[1] In simpler terms, a principle is a self-evident truth.

I give my students an example like this: If a person sets a goal to get a perfect score on the ACT exam and graduate with a 4.0 GPA but misses classes on a regular basis, rarely studies, and doesn't engage in the classroom, then that person is really not *aligned* with a realistic chance of achieving that goal. Therefore, that individual's actions don't match up with the goal. The students all understand that line of reasoning. I then briefly go through some of the goals that were stated, and we discuss what would be properly aligned actions and behaviors to give those individuals a realistic chance of accomplishing their goal. I close this part of the discussion by telling them that when they return home, they should sit down with their parents to share the goals they've articulated and then come up with an action plan together.

This is, in essence, the key to the principle of alignment. When your children's actions and behaviors are out of alignment with their goals, they have two choices: they can change their goal *or* they can change their behavior. It's really that simple.

Now, the part that is a bit trickier is that in order for the principle of alignment to work, there needs to be an *alignment specialist* involved. Now that you've helped your child find an interest and set some goals, the day-to-day effort (siege) of becoming an alignment specialist begins. In helping our children become the best THEY can be, our knowledge, wisdom, life experience, stability, and resolve are what they need now. They need someone to help keep them aligned with their goals in the same way we take our car to the garage and have an expert mechanic check that the car is properly aligned and in working order. They need someone to help them understand the cause-and-effect relationship between big dreams and big goals and realistically aligning themselves to achieving those goals with their day-to-day and week-to-week actions and behavior. They need someone to step in when they lose sight of the big picture. They need an alignment specialist who can help them decide to change their goals or change their behaviors as needed. Are you ready to become an alignment specialist? If so, buckle up. You're in for a ride!

NOTES

1. Dictionary.com, s.v. "principle," accessed March 6, 2015, http://dictionary.reference.com/browse/principle.

LIFE LESSON #6

BECOMING AN ALIGNMENT SPECIALIST

"Always bear in mind that your own resolution to succeed is more important than any other."[1]

—Abraham Lincoln

The *principle of alignment* states that when you are not properly aligned with a realistic chance of accomplishing your goal, you have two options:

You can change your goal.

OR

You can change your actions and behavior to more fully align with your goals.

With more life experience to pull from, we parents tend to more readily see the big picture. So, it's our job to keep our kids on track—reminding them that our job is to help them achieve THEIR goals. You will see the words *their* and *they* capitalized throughout this book because understanding this concept is the most critical part of being an alignment specialist: be cautious not to hijack you child's goals by replacing them with your own. Remember, your children's goals are their goals, not yours. You are the alignment specialist. When they are out of alignment, a reminder that they can either change their goal or change their behavior is in order. Giving that reminder and then helping them to get back on track is what makes you as a parent their alignment specialist.

Right now, you may be thinking this philosophy of being an alignment specialist is no more than just words on a page or an abstract concept. It may seem like a nice idea, but there is nothing concrete about it yet. It is a nebulous, gray area and not much help in its current state. My wife is an avid reader of parenting books, and she often grows frustrated with the absence of any "real life" help to elucidate such concepts. She is the type of reader who always wants to know the "how" of an idea. *But how can I put this into practice with my own children? What will this look like in my own family?* This won't be a comprehensive how-to list, but I would like to elaborate on the idea and illustrate *how* my wife and I have tried to become alignment specialists in the lives of our children.

To start off, this principle must be explained in context of good, better, and best—a concept taught by Latter-day Saint leader Dallin H. Oaks—which states that while some choices are good, others are better, and some are best. The trick is to understand the difference and then choose best opportunities as often as possible.[2] Our children are faced with a plethora, a veritable smorgasbord, of "good" and "better" decisions on a daily—sometimes hourly—basis. It is incumbent upon us to draw on our extra years to help our children learn to make the absolute "best" decisions in terms of alignment with their respective goals. This is a daily siege. We must have stiff backbones, resolve, and the energy necessary to be unwavering in our role. Our children may be resistant at times, but we can have confidence in the principle and take responsibility to keep them aligned with THEIR goals.

Before I give some examples, let me explain a key point. After I spoke on this topic at a BYU alumni function, one father made the observation that what he could see with the alignment specialist concept was that it takes a lot of the emotion out of the equation and takes the parent out of the role of being the enforcer (the bad guy) in the relationship. Instead, a parent becomes the facilitator (the good guy)—someone who is in the child's corner and has his or her best interests at heart. When the child understands that the parent is truly and sincerely trying to help, rather than just being a strict and rigid disciplinarian, the relationship dynamic changes for the better for both parent and child.

Another thing to keep in mind is that implementation of this principle has to be fluid. Your children's goals, circumstances, and desires are dynamic and changing. The important thing is that changes or adjustments should not be made in the heat (or emotion) of a moment—when friends are pulling in one direction, when the child is licking wounds from a disappointing loss, or when hitting the books just doesn't seem very fun. When changes or deviations from a certain goal need to be made or new goals are set because of changing interests, it is important to be flexible in sitting down with our children to understand where they are coming from. When things have cooled down, we can help guide them to make proper adjustments or direction changes. Long story short—don't try to make these major course alterations while your child is dealing with disappointments, setbacks, or distractions.

I'll illustrate how this can be a changing and evolving process. Our two older sons, John and Matthew, decided that they wanted to play professional tennis, and they made huge sacrifices when they were in elementary school in order to align themselves with this goal. They missed out on countless friends' birthday parties and a myriad of other "kid things" because they practiced every morning and afternoon, often traveled on weekends, and then had to catch up on homework from missing school with any extra time. They were aligned, striving toward their goal, and seeing success along the way. One morning, however, John woke up blind in one eye. The doctors attributed this to an autoimmune disease that attacked his optic nerve and caused significant swelling. He was diagnosed with optic neuritis, and it was determined that the best treatment to save his eye was to bombard his system with steroids. One of the potential side effects of these high-dose steroid treatments, especially during these years of growth and development, is that normal growth patterns could be curbed. While he eventually recovered most of his sight (he still has a small blind spot in the one eye), the doctors do believe he lost a few inches of height from the heavy doses of steroids.

After this experience, we sat down with John in the role of alignment specialists and helped him rethink some of his previous goals. He came to the conclusion that it was unlikely for him to make a living in a sport that has become dominated by ever bigger and stronger athletes. Despite his childhood dream, he felt that he would have too much of a physical disadvantage. So he made a course correction. He decided that his new ticket to the kind of life he wanted was a combination of tennis and academics in college, and he changed his plans and goals to reflect this new direction in his life. (This was an example of choosing to change the goal, because John himself came to the conclusion that it was no longer realistically achievable.)

While on the same professional track early on, Matthew's story played out a little differently. Unlike John, he didn't have anything forced upon him that necessitated a direction change. Matthew had simply changed his personal desires. As he grew up, he decided he wanted to follow in the footsteps of his older siblings and focus more on becoming a superb student athlete. As alignment specialists, my wife and I were there to counsel, guide, and direct, and we could see that this wasn't a heat-of-the-moment decision, but rather a change of heart. So his goals became more aligned with his brother's again. (This was an example of Matthew choosing to change his goal because of a change in personal desire and interest.)

The point is that our children's goals change and evolve on a regular basis, so we need to be flexible and discriminate between changes in direction made because of real and changing circumstances and those changes made because of the lack of big-picture perspective.

Let me share a few more examples illustrating the job of an alignment specialist. Our oldest daughter, Jordan, set a long-term goal that she wanted to earn—through academic merit and extracurricular activity—the Gordon B. Hinckley presidential scholarship at BYU. This was one of her primary goals from a young age, and it meant that she had to be an excellent student to even apply for this scholarship.

There was a time when Jordan was nervous about an important test for an AP class. From calculating it out, she knew she had to do really well in order to keep an A in the class. However, the evening before the test, she had planned on attending a school function that she had helped organize as the head cheerleader. It was something she was looking forward to and was excited about. She also felt some responsibility to attend. No one would argue that the event didn't sound like a lot of fun or that it wasn't a "good" thing to attend. But the risk she ran from eliminating all of her study time on this *particular* evening was that she might not score as well on the test, potentially dropping her grade in the class, lowering her GPA, and jeopardizing her goal of earning the Hinckley scholarship. Was skipping studying for the exam to go to this *particular* evening's event an action aligned with her long-term goal? Probably not. So when we saw her preparing to leave, what did we do as alignment specialists? We called her aside and initiated a discussion. "Jordan, is going to this function tonight really the best thing you can do with your time? Or do you think you should be studying for your test? If you don't get an A on this test, can you still get an A in the class? If you don't get an A in this class, will it still be possible for you to be a legitimate candidate for a presidential scholarship?" Like every teenager, she moaned and groaned, insisting that she would be fine and adding something to the effect that "isn't an A– good enough?" We told her that an A– in this class was a great accomplishment. It was a hard class. But that was not her goal. And it was our job to remind her of that, so we did. Was she happy about it? No, not that night. She had dozens of other opportunities to enjoy relaxing and having fun in her capacity as a cheerleader but only one chance to prepare well for that test. And years later, when the Hinckley Scholarship had given her an extra $30,000 to help her through school, then yes. *Then* she was really happy about our intervention in that decision. (This was an example of Jordan's choosing to change actions and behavior that particular night in order to be aligned with her long-term goals.)

Through the years, it was tough to hold our ground in such situations. (Might I suggest the purchase of a helmet and flak jacket?) Our resolve, however, came from the fact that we decided our children were counting on us. Whether they liked it or not, whether they knew it or not, they needed us to be alignment specialists to hold them accountable to THEIR goals. Even the most highly motivated kids need someone to keep them on track from time to time.

Let me share another example to drive home this concept. Our son John had set a goal to attend a top-level university through a combination of academic and athletic scholarships and was on track to achieve this goal at the end of his senior year. Similar to Jordan, John had a conflict that arose with a worthwhile activity that would cut into his study time the night before a big test in a demanding science course. John had little margin for error because of his goals—goals that he had worked toward for a long time and was almost at the finish line. Because he was a teenager and was thinking like a teenager, like Jordan and Tara before him, he was headed out the door for this more appealing activity rather than buckling down to do the hard work in preparing for a difficult test. Before he could get out the door, we started our communication with him with questions similar to the questions we had asked his sister years earlier. We ultimately prevailed in getting him to see how the one decision of attending an activity (albeit worthwhile) that wasn't aligned with a major long-term goal of his was not the "best" decision as to how he spent his time that particular night.

As the months went by, we may have given a few gentle reminders, but we were mostly able to observe him choose "best" decisions in how he prioritized his time in aligning with his goals. We knew that college and a Church mission were around the corner for him, so our opportunities to teach him about proper alignment with goals and time management would shortly be coming to an end because he would be on his own. Our window to prepare him for college and a mission was closing. As a senior who was close to the finish line, John had learned the principle of alignment very well and was making very good decisions, but he still needed some guidance from time to time. We didn't want him to blow all that he had worked for in his final semester, so we remained vigilant and on guard. It is exactly these kind of situations where our children need some guidance and direction.

Latter-day Saint leader Quentin L. Cook had this to say on the subject of choices and priorities in a recent general conference address:

> My concern is not only about the big tipping-point decisions but also the middle ground—the workaday world and seemingly ordinary decisions where we spend most of our time. In these areas, we need to emphasize moderation, balance, and especially wisdom. It is important to rise above rationalizations and make the best choices. . . . I believe Elder Dallin H. Oaks's inspired message distinguishing between "good, better, best" provides an effective way to evaluate choices and priorities. Many choices are not inherently evil, but if they absorb all of our time and keep us from the best choices, then they become insidious. Even worthwhile endeavors need evaluation in order to determine if they have become distractions from the best goals. I had a memorable discussion with my father when I was a teenager. He did not believe enough young people were focused on or preparing for long-term important goals—like employment and providing for families. Meaningful study and preparatory work experience were always at the top of my father's recommended priorities."[3]

In John's case, his making a seemingly good decision, but perhaps not the best decision, could have ended up costing him important opportunities in his future and tens of thousands of dollars in scholarship money. Instead, this experience helped him to make better, more prioritized decisions in proper context of long-term goals. So what's the point of this story? The point is that while this singular decision might not have had any significant consequences, there were plenty of decisions coming the next day, the next week, and the next month that might.

These are just a few examples of decisions that our teenagers make every day. We can help them discern the absolute best decisions from the better and good decisions. Even more than that, we need to be helping them see *when* the best decisions are absolutely critical so they aren't jeopardizing their futures and limiting options along the way. The idea is that acting *consistently* in the role of an alignment specialist will help our children learn to make daily decisions that are fully aligned with their goals and in context of the big picture when we're not around. That's why we as parents rely on good judgment and inspiration in guiding our children to make the "best" decisions—in "wisdom and order"—and in accord with the counsel of ecclesiastical leaders, both past and present (see Mosiah 4:27).

One somewhat tangential, yet important, item that I want to add to these examples is the importance of keeping the communication lines open. Now, don't think that life in the Pearce family is the same as a day in the life of the Cleavers,' because it's not. There are a lot of colorful personalities in our family, which means that our family culture is quite lively. We are pretty open with each other, we have a lot of inside jokes, and we have been accused on occasion of having our own "Pearce language." That works for us just as your family culture works for you. This is as it should be. Cindi and I have found that open and real communication is a very important part of positively influencing—teaching, helping, training, coaching—our children through their teenage years.

We all want our children to have balance in their lives, so things can get really tricky when it comes to weighing time spent in Church assignments, social activities, academic and athletic pursuits, and the pursuit of music and the arts. With good organization, prioritization, and communication, we can teach our children that there is enough time to find balance and serve all of these worthy goals and pursuits while magnifying those that are the most important—and still have some fun. But it's not easy. We must rely and trust that we will use good judgment in guiding our children and that we are entitled to inspiration in the process.

I could go on and on with specific examples that have come up on a daily basis with all of our children where we've had to help them discriminate between good, better, and best decisions in context of how they spend their time and whether that time spent is aligned with their goals. Let me assure you that if you're involved in the goal-setting process with each of your children and are committed to the idea that it is your role as the parent to keep them aligned with their goals, through time and practice you will become an alignment specialist. As your children realize goals and dreams that they never thought possible, they will come to thank you for it. Those are the sweet moments that will make all of the difficult, unpleasant times worth it. In the meantime, gird up your loins, fresh courage take, and I wasn't kidding about the helmet and flak jacket. But take heart! There's nothing that will replace the moment when a few years of hindsight will lead a child back to say "thank you."

Think of it in these terms: Our goal as parents in teaching and helping our children to become the best they can be starts with us in the role of alignment specialists. When our children start to figure things out and make the best decisions on their own (in full alignment with their stated goals), then we move from the passenger seat to the back seat. *(I call back seat, middle, feet on the hump!)* Then we can begin to enjoy the ride as we see our children accomplish things that likely would have exceeded their grasp if we hadn't been there for them when they needed someone with a stiff backbone and a fully developed frontal lobe.

The secret is in getting our children to set THEIR goals and then for us, as parents, to hold them accountable to those goals as alignment specialists until such a time that a legitimate course correction needs to be made due to changing circumstances. We are preparing them to become "agents unto themselves" (see D&C 58:28), but right now they are teenagers.

Whatever the pursuit, we do this by simply being the person in the room that points out when some realignment needs to happen. Sometimes this reminder also needs the disclaimer that this is their goal, life, and future. They aren't doing this for us. They are doing it for themselves. Whether they decide to change their behavior or change their goal, it is still theirs to own. I am often asked, "When does our role as an alignment specialist end?" I believe the answer is that our role changes as our children get older and become more responsible for their own lives. I liken it to Newton's inverse square law of gravity. When our children's responsibility over their own lives and ownership of their decisions grows, ours shrinks.

Becoming an alignment specialist is not easy. In fact, it's very hard. It's quite often exhausting. And sometimes it feels like a veritable siege. So I don't want to have you read this and think, *How easy! Any parent can do this!* While the concept is easy enough to understand, putting it into practice on a consistent basis is difficult. Teenagers will test us at all hours of the day and night when we are at our weakest—when it has been the longest week ever full of projects at work, church assignments, volunteer work, PTA assignments, illnesses, never-ending lists, and—quite frankly—we have no desire for yet another energy-draining conversation. It is at these times that spouses will need to back each other up and most likely implement a tag-team approach. But if we are committed to the principle of alignment with our children and practice it no matter how difficult it can be, our children will get a lot closer to achieving their goals than if we simply let them learn through trial and error. They will eventually learn through trial and error and through the School of Hard Knocks, but the opportunity cost of that kind of an education can be an impediment.

While there is no substitute for spiritual enlightenment in helping our children make the best possible decisions in context of their worthwhile short- and long-term goals, I submit to you that becoming an expert alignment specialist can help us all to teach our children to become the best THEY can be—the end goal of becoming a certified alignment specialist.

NOTES

1. Abraham Lincoln to Isham Reavis, 5 November, 1855, "Lincoln's Advice to Lawyers," Abraham Lincoln Online, accessed March 9, 2015, http://www.abrahamlincolnonline.org/lincoln/speeches/law.htm.

2. Dallin H. Oaks, "Good, Better, Best," October 2007, accessed March 9, 2015, https://www.lds.org/general-conference/2007/10/good-better-best?lang=eng.

3. Quentin L. Cook, "Choose Wisely," October 2014, accessed March 9, 2015, https://www.lds.org/general-conference/2014/10/choose-wisely?lang=eng.

WE'RE NOT TRYING TO LOSE THIS MATCH

"Our greatest weakness lies in giving up. The most certain way to succeed is always to try just one more time."

—Attributed to Thomas Edison

Throughout my career, there were plenty of times that I had to be determined to win. I felt that no obstacle or challenge was too great, and I had the satisfaction of walking off the court knowing I had given my absolute all. My son John quipped after one such particularly grueling and remarkable comeback win in his own junior career, "I wasn't trying to lose that match." That phrase took on a life of its own and was ever after used in our family as a way of conveying that absolutely nothing was going to get in the way of prevailing in a high-stakes, high-pressure situation, no matter the arena—classroom, tennis court, sacrament meeting talk, or prom. Anything that was a high-pressure situation, where clowning-out could occur, suddenly fell under this umbrella expression. John may have coined this term, but ironically, it was John who gave Cindi and me the toughest match of our parenting life through his freshman and sophomore years of high school. We had to double-team him with the determination that "we weren't going to lose this match." *This match* being a phase of life during which he lost his ambition to excel academically and took up a stubborn insistence that it would not make a difference to his future.

As I've given seminars, I've gotten this question a lot over the years, "So what do you do when your kid is not motivated or is lacking ambition to work toward anything? Do you just force them or what?" In *living* this scenario with John and school, Cindi and I had to counsel together to decide on a game plan. We knew that we didn't want to see our son take a few missteps early on and then pay dear consequences the rest of his life. Eventually, we decided that in order to not lose this match, we had to be mentally tougher than John and step in to save him from himself. We believed very strongly in this approach and went to work, hoping John would eventually come around. "My job is to save you from yourself until you know better" quickly became another oft-touted Pearce family credo. (And yes, our children have made it quite clear they are looking forward to the day with great anticipation when they can step in to save us from our elderly stricken selves.)

As far as implementation of this philosophy is concerned, I don't necessarily think there is one right answer or method in this. You could go with force, punishment, reward, or a combination of all the above. Let me suggest one other option—leverage. As this situation played out with John, Cindi and I found that leverage was our best bet to not lose this match.

My wife knew that two things were important to John—playing tennis tournaments and hanging out with his friends on the weekends when he was in town. So she used these two things as leverage in striking a deal with him. The terms were as follows: as long as John kept all As in his classes, he could continue to practice tennis, play tournaments, and spend time with his friends on weekends. For John, Fridays became a day of reckoning. He would come home from school and sit down with Cindi at the kitchen computer to check his grades. If he had all As, he could go out with friends, and Cindi would sign him up for the tennis tournaments with entry dates the following week. If he didn't have all As, he couldn't go out with friends, and Cindi didn't sign him up for the upcoming tennis tournaments. It was that simple.

Of course, writing this is your quintessential "easier said than done." Cindi now laughs how this period was so challenging. It was a day-to-day siege with John! Now don't get the wrong idea—John was a great kid. He never got into any kind of trouble, was making good decisions in his personal life, and was a leader in his quorum and carrying out Church responsibilities. He was simply going through a phase where he had temporarily lost his ambition to excel academically. However, with Cindi's leadership, we worked together and combined our strength, resolve, and mental toughness to wear him down and save him from himself. We weren't going to lose that match! And sure enough, by the time John got to his junior year, he had had a complete paradigm shift. All he could talk about was grades, academic scholarships, Ivy League requirements, graduate schools, and so on. It was a complete turnaround.

The rest of the story is that because of his academic, leadership, and tennis achievements, John was recruited by Harvard, Princeton, Columbia, Notre Dame, and BYU. After they each paid for official recruiting trips to their campuses, he chose BYU, accepting a full academic scholarship as well as an athletic scholarship in tennis. While he ended up deciding BYU was the best fit for him, the important thing in all of this was that he had a lot of good options because his mom refused to let him lose a "critical match" during a temporary teenage phase.

He lived in the dorms his freshman year, so while I saw him every day at tennis practice and for matches, he was pretty much on his own as far as school was concerned. After a summer, fall, winter, and spring at BYU, he left on a mission, having been successful in the classroom, on the court, and in a leadership role in representing our team on the Cougar Council. Somewhere along the line, he had found his own intrinsic motivation. No further parental saving required. *We didn't lose that match.*

In teaching our children to become the best THEY can be, sometimes we simply need to save them from themselves until they can figure it out. John needed a little saving from his own stubbornness until *he* figured out that maybe he did want a future with some options. And since we had stepped in with our leverage game plan, he still had viable options when he finally did come around. In this case with our son John, we chose the right method and had the necessary resolve to "not lose this match."

LIFE LESSON #8

FAMILY CULTURE

"The family is both the fundamental unit of society as well as the root of culture. It . . . is a perpetual source of encouragement, advocacy, assurance, and emotional refueling that empowers a child to venture with confidence into the greater world and to become all that he can be."[1]

—Marianne E. Neifert

I am a product of a goal-oriented family culture. While there were obvious competitive advantages in my siblings and me pursuing tennis, since my father was a tennis coach and former Utah tennis great, my parents didn't necessarily push us that direction. All of us eventually gravitated toward it. They did, however, care that we were always productive in the pursuit of worthwhile endeavors. To be clear—playing video games or watching television after school were not part of what they considered "worthwhile pursuits." This kind of a family culture—where we were taught to set goals and work productively toward achieving them—is what helped me check the boxes along the way.

Creating your own family culture is nothing more than creating a picture collage, if you will, of what things your family will focus on. It provides a framework for what makes you unique and distinct as a family. It will help you feel bonded and act as a cohesive force. It has for us. Cindi and I determined early on that we had a few things we wanted to become part of our family culture: 1) balance, 2) hard work and play—no "dancing through life," 3) responsibility to live up to your individual potential, 4) focus on academics, 5) understanding and appreciation of the value of work and finances, 6) some background and skills in music and the arts (or at least an appreciation for them), 7) involvement in a sport, 8) testimonies and faithful service in Church callings, and 9) laughter and a sense of humor.

Since you may have thought the last item was a bit out of place, let me explain our intent in including this as part of our culture. We wanted our kids to learn how to laugh, not take themselves too seriously, and find the humor in everyday life. So we really encouraged and whooped it up, so to speak, when we thought they were being funny! Now, if you came to dinner, you might not think we're funny in the least. The important thing is that *we* think we're funny. As a result—our kids truly enjoy spending time together as a family. So laughing, or being funny in and of itself wasn't really the goal; it was forming tight-knit relationships and being able to draw strength from a sense of family closeness.

Along with establishing traits and characteristics that we wanted to emphasize in our home, we decided that it was important to establish clear expectations for our kids. We wanted our kids to know what we expected of them. Our kids knew those expectations, but they also knew that they could expect us, as parents, to support them and help provide them with the necessary resources to meet those expectations.

Whatever you choose to do or not do, your family culture is of your *own* making, and creating a family culture can help you narrow down what you want your family to be all about. Our family culture is constantly evolving and is a work in progress. While neither perfect nor perfectly executed, we do have a framework that helps our family stay centered and focused on what we're all about. I expect that your family culture will be unique and different from ours. I'm sure it reflects those things that are valued and appreciated in your home.

Now, you may be asking, how on earth did having a family culture help me get to Centre Court at Wimbledon, and more importantly, how can it help you teach your children to become the best THEY can be? The family culture that I came from—being goal oriented—helped me to stay on track through the many years it took slogging away in practice and in competition to become really good at something. I knew what I was about, I knew what my goals were, and I was pursuing them with my parents encouraging me every step of the way. I never questioned the direction I was going, the time spent, or the sacrifices that were made, because it's just what we did and what I was taught to do. Relentlessly and tirelessly pursuing our goals was the norm; it was part of our family culture.

Our family culture has incorporated what Cindi and I felt were the best things from each of our own families, as well as adopting some things from other families we admired; we formed our own value system as to how we would raise our children. This is the value of great neighbors and neighborhoods, schools, good friends, churches, and positive adult role models. As the expression goes, "imitation is the sincerest form of flattery," and the tenets that laid the foundation of our family culture came from our own upbringings and our rubbing shoulders and being influenced by good people along the way.

In getting back to the issue of how your family culture can help your children to become the best THEY can be, it will be your family culture that will provide a foundation and a framework to help your children stay focused on those things that are of value within your home. When your family culture and expectations become more clearly defined, it will come to be just what you do. And furthermore, it will become not just what you do but will come to define who you are as a family and who your children are as individuals. As Kipling wrote, "For the strength of the Pack is the Wolf, and the strength of the Wolf is the Pack."[2] So it is with our families. Developing a family culture together, setting clearly defined expectations and providing the necessary resources for those expectations to be met can help your children to become the best THEY can be—which is the goal we're all striving for as parents. Ask yourselves what you want your family culture to be like and what some of the attributes of your family culture would be. Answering these questions will help you get a jump start in developing your own family culture.

Jot down some thoughts about your own family's culture and what you'd like it to be

_____

_____

_____

_____

_____

_____

_____

_____

_____

_____

_____

_____

_____

_____

_____

_____

_____

_____

_____

_____

_____

_____

_____

_____

_____

_____

_____

_____

_____

_____

NOTES

1. Marianne E. Neifert, _Dr. Mom's Parenting Guide: Common-Sense Guidance for the Life of Your Child_ (New York: Plume, 1996).

2. Rudyard Kipling, _The Second Jungle Book_ (New York: The Century Co., 1895), 29.

LIFE LESSON #9

OUR REACH
EXCEEDS OUR GRASP

*"Ah, but a man's reach should exceed
his grasp, or what's a Heaven for?"* [1]

—Robert Browning

I've chosen this line from Robert Browning's poem to start this lesson because it teaches us in goal-setting to extend as far as our "reach" can take us, even though we may never "grasp" the ultimate goal.

Let me illustrate. I start off by telling my students during my goal-setting seminar at BYU tennis camps that one of my goals when I was about their age (teenage) was to win Wimbledon. While I had many boxes to check along the way (which we've already covered) to reach this ultimate goal, winning Wimbledon had always been something that kept me awake at night. This provides a perfect lead-in to a discussion about setting their goals high—to reach for the stars, as Browning suggests.

I point out that by setting my goal very high (my "reach") to win Wimbledon, I probably got a lot further than I otherwise would have if I had simply set a goal to get into the main draw at Wimbledon or win the first round at Wimbledon. This is where they really start paying attention, so I say something like this: "While winning Wimbledon was my dream or reach goal, and I dedicated and aligned to give myself a realistic chance of achieving it, I didn't accomplish it." What I then say is that I failed at accomplishing this goal in my life, but I don't consider myself a failure and probably got further and accomplished more than if I had set a less lofty goal!

This is what Cindi and I have taught our children, and it's what I teach my players and campers—that coming up a little short in something does not make you a failure. Sure, they may not grasp the ultimate prize, in the same way I didn't win Wimbledon, but as long as they were doing everything in their power to reach for it, they are true champions and certainly not failures. As we teach our children to set goals and work to achieve them by aligning their behavior and actions to give themselves a realistic chance of checking that box, affirm that it's okay to shoot for the stars because, as Browning said, our reach will often exceed our grasp. They'll get farther and accomplish more along the way than they otherwise would have.

NOTES

1. Robert Browning, "Andrea del Sarto," *Men and Women* (Boston: Ticknor and Fields 1856), 187.

LIFE LESSON #10

EMBRACE THE DEFINING MOMENTS

"From what we get, we can make a living;
what we give, however, makes a life."

—Attributed to Arthur Ashe

Embrace those moments when your child takes ownership over the direction of his or her life and goals.

I was enjoying being a typical high school student during my sophomore year: going to football games on weekends with friends, starting to date, and being a member of the basketball team. Socially, playing high school tennis wasn't really that big of a deal, but being a member of the basketball team seemed pretty cool at the time.

Official basketball practice started around October, and the season didn't end until March, just about the time high school tennis started. Practices were immediately following school, went for a couple of hours, and were exhausting. While I tried to work in some tennis before school and sometimes tried to get a hit after practice in the evenings, between schoolwork, being a teenager and needing sleep, and the physicality of basketball practice and games, I was usually too tired to be very productive with tennis. Tennis, according to my childhood dreams and goals, was supposed to be my focus, but it was becoming an afterthought as I was pursuing my basketball career and the newfound glory of being on the sophomore team.

As I am now a parent of six children, I applaud my parents and their patience in letting me pursue my hoop dreams, knowing that at my size of 5'9" and an average vertical, basketball was not going to be my ticket to a college scholarship or to the pros. As my tennis and national ranking went by the wayside, my parents came to all of my games and were always very supportive of me and the team. It must have been hard for them, but they never showed it.

One day, I recall my father having a conversation with me. I now call it a "reality check" about what I thought my chances were of earning a college scholarship and then moving on into the pro game if I were to stay with basketball as my chosen sport. He brought up my height and asked me how many pros at my height were playing the game at the pro level, let alone at the collegiate level. What he was asking me to consider sunk in.

We discussed other things along the lines of a typical reality-check conversation between father and son, and as I look back, he handled it very well. My ego wasn't bruised. He didn't discourage me from continuing to play basketball, he was just making some "observations" that he would like me to consider. Well, basketball season finally ended in March, and I picked up my tennis racket, dusted it off, and went back to playing tennis. I really hadn't played that much tennis in almost six months, and I was incredibly rusty. Nevertheless, I was still good enough that I had a successful high school season. I won state individually at the number one singles position and led our team to a state championship.

As summer came and went, my results at the national level, which really mattered in terms of the college recruitment process, were lackluster. After some reflection, it was downright frustrating to me that I was losing to players that I knew I had the potential to beat. However, the reality was that my national peers were practicing 365 days of the year, 3–4 hours a day (even more if you were at an academy like Bollettieri's in Florida) and playing tournaments every weekend. While they were doing that, I was logging time on the basketball court working on my ball-handling skills, jump shots, and free throws. It was obvious after a summer of national tournaments that I had fallen behind.

As a college tennis coach himself, my dad always said that the results from your junior year of high school were what really mattered in terms of college recruitment. He felt that the smart coaches didn't pay much attention to the rankings in the sixteen-and-under age group, figuring that with different rates of maturity, some boys had gained their height and strength earlier than others and had overwhelming physical advantages that eventually evened out in the older age group. So I was coming up on my key year—the all-important junior year of high school—and if I wanted to get the attention of a school like UCLA that had won fifteen national titles and been the proving grounds of players like Arthur Ashe and Jimmy Connors, I had some thinking to do. Moreover, if I was going to align myself with a realistic chance of achieving my childhood dream of winning Wimbledon, I had an important, defining-moment decision to make. Was I going to continue playing basketball or devote my time to tennis during my junior of high school?

What it came down to was the feeling that I wasn't living up to my potential, and my childhood dreams of becoming a professional tennis player and winning Wimbledon seemed like just that, a dream, with no basis in reality. So just before school was about to start, my crucial junior year, I went to my parents and told them that I wasn't going to play basketball anymore, and that I was going to devote myself to tennis. They were supportive of this decision and applauded my maturity. But I wasn't done. I then added that in order to be the best that I could be, I felt I needed to move to California so I could get great practice against better competition on a daily basis and play tournaments every weekend. They were shocked at this dramatic and somewhat extreme declaration of what I was committed and prepared to do—all in order to be the best that I could be. This became my defining moment. This was when I took my first real step, by my own accord, to fully align myself with a realistic chance of achieving my childhood dreams and goals. At the age of sixteen, barely legal and not really qualified to drive a car, I was asking my parents to send me away from my family and friends so I could fully dedicate myself to becoming the best tennis player I could be. This was a sacrifice of monumental proportions, but I believed at the time that this was what was required for me to be fully aligned with a realistic chance of achieving my goals. As they say in poker, I was "all in!"

Defining moments are those points in time when our children, perhaps after months or even years of our pushing, prodding, cajoling, and even driving them at times, finally take ownership of their own goals and future. Like us, you're probably going to have to win some "tough matches" to get to this point, but hold out for these moments, and never give up hope they will eventually happen—that moment, for the first time, when you can move from the driver's seat over to the passenger's seat and enjoy the ride. When these moments come, it makes all of your efforts, patience, head-banging, and hand-wringing worth it, so stay the course and keep being the best teacher you can be. Those defining moments will come, and when they do, embrace them!

LIFE LESSON #11

SACRIFICE

*"To give anything less than your
best is to sacrifice the gift."*[1]

—Steve Prefontaine

While my sacrifice to be the best that I could be was on the extreme end of the sacrifice scale as a teenager, I'm grateful to my parents for embracing my defining moment and supporting me. As Frost said in "The Road Not Taken," "that has made all the difference."[2]

I don't really teach the kind of sacrifice I made to become the best that I could be during my seminars because it's pretty extreme. However, it's important that we encourage and support the sacrifices that our children make in context of our family values and culture. The key is that whatever sacrifices are made come from their taking ownership over their future, not the parent forcing them into something they don't really want or lack the commitment to do. I've already discussed my defining moment in deciding to move to California and become a full-time dedicated tennis player. The defining moment was the decision and a point of time where I was now taking responsibility for my own goals and future. This principle, of course, can be applied to any pursuit or endeavor. However, it was the sacrifice that followed that helped me to reach my goals of becoming number one in the country as a junior tennis player, earn a scholarship to UCLA, and enjoy a successful pro career.

When I told my parents what I wanted to do, they were initially shocked, but to their credit they took me seriously. To this day, I don't know what they discussed with each other, but I left it in their hands to find the best possible solution to what I wanted to do. I ended up moving in with a family that had a son my age who was also a nationally prominent tennis player.

When we were both twelve years old, we had both needed doubles partners at the National Claycourt Championships for twelve and under held in Winston-Salem, North Carolina, so we paired up together. We ended up winning the doubles title together even though we'd never met or ever played tennis with each other before. Our pick-up partnership led to a national championship.

Somehow my parents thought way back to this event, remembering that this young man and his family lived in Rolling Hills Estates (Palos Verdes), California, and played tennis at the famous Jack Kramer Club. This particular club, at the time, had become a hotbed of junior tennis talent. They had hired a very dynamic teaching pro who had become a magnet for junior tennis talent from around the country, so there were not only the kids whose families actually lived in the area but also a few like me who were boarding with families to increase the talent pool.

So arrangements were made for me to live with this family, go to Miraleste High School in Palos Verdes, and become a junior tennis member at the Jack Kramer Club. It's hard to believe that I actually made and stood by this decision. My aunt Janice, fearing for my safety as a sixteen-year-old driver in the "fast lane" of southern California roads and traffic, donated to me the biggest car ever made—the Oldsmobile, Delta 88 ("The Boat"). This car got eight miles to the gallon, was maroon and enormously long, and had a trunk that was spacious enough to live in. This was my urban assault vehicle, provided solely for my safety.

On a fall day in September 1982, my Delta 88 was packed up, and I was leaving family and friends and moving to California. (My dad drove down with me and then flew back home.) I still remember my first time on the 405 freeway at the end of our trip to Palos Verdes. I'm sure my dad still remembers it too, because it was harrowing with me at the wheel.

My first day of school was hilarious—right out of the movies. Palos Verdes and Miraleste High School was comparable to *Beverly Hills 90210*, so picture me pulling into school the first day: a kid from Provo, Utah, in his aunt's Delta 88 amongst teenagers driving the finest of cars. This was definitely not Timpview's parking lot in 1982. After the initial trauma of moving in my junior year of high school to a new school with only one person I knew who I could call a friend, I eventually settled into a routine.

And this is what made me. That's why I would say in teaching your children to be the best THEY can be, allowing them to make sacrifices (perhaps not as dramatic as mine) can be a good thing and make all the difference. It did for me. The sole purpose of the move was to be in an environment where I had plenty of practice partners, court time, good weather, and tournaments every weekend. Since my mom and dad weren't there for me (I was on my own), it was up to me to get myself to school, get my homework done, work things out with teachers, set my practice schedule, and enter and drive myself to tournaments on the weekends all over southern California. Every Sunday evening, I would get on the phone and call my tennis peers and set up practice matches for the week. It would go something like this, "Hey, Eric, how about Monday at three o'clock?" and so on until every day of the work week was filled with a practice match. Weekends were reserved for tournaments.

Sacrifice teaches responsibility, resourcefulness, and initiative—attributes that are imperative for success.

If I didn't make the phone calls, organize my week, reserve the courts, get my homework done, study for tests, focus during practice sessions, and so on, it simply didn't happen. Although I was living with a family and they were very kind, supportive, and a great help to me, it was up to me to make sure I was doing things on a daily basis on the court and in the classroom to make my extreme sacrifice worth it. Fortunately, it did.

After a semester of living at Palos Verdes and playing at the Kramer Club, I relocated to Orange County and settled in with the Whittingham family, whose son Fred was one of my best friends growing up in our elementary school days. I continued doing the same things in this new environment, dutifully practicing against the best competition in the country (even the world back then) and playing tournaments on weekends. The following summer I took fifth place at the biggest national tournament of the year as a seventeen-year-old in my first year in the eighteen-and-under division. And I still had another year, my senior year, to make the jump from number five to number one and reach my goal of becoming the best junior tennis player in the country, which I later accomplished.

To this day, I am grateful for the kindness and generosity of the families who took me in. But as I look back, it was still a tough year being away from my own family. You may ask, "Was it worth it?" Absolutely. As I mentioned before, it made me. I learned to take responsibility for myself and my dreams and goals, and I learned along the way important life skills, such as organization, resourcefulness, initiative, resilience, diligence, discipline, and persistence, which are all necessary to realize success. Because this experience was so profound in my life, Cindi and I have taught our children at the earliest of ages to take responsibility and make sacrifices for their dreams and goals in keeping with our family values and culture.

Fast-forward to my sophomore year at UCLA. After a somewhat unsuccessful summer playing professional tournaments as a member of the USTA Collegiate Davis Cup Team, I determined that in order to turn pro and get out doing what I wanted to do (be a professional tennis player), I needed to win the Adidas Invitational in the fall. This was a collegiate event, but the significance of it was that the winner got a main-draw wild card into the Pilot Pen Classic—the precursor to today's BNP Paribas Open held in Indian Wells, California. Many refer to this tournament today as the fifth Grand Slam. It was a big professional tournament with a lot of valuable ranking points associated with each win. This was my primary goal for the fall of 1985, so I put together a game plan to prepare myself as best I could to win this tournament and earn the wildcard.

Since I was a student athlete with a full academic load of classes, I had to manage my time really well to fit in everything I felt was important to be fully prepared for victory. The first thing I did was meet with one of UCLA's strength and conditioning coaches to put together a program specifically for me in addition to what we did every day at team practice. This is standard in tennis programs at universities across the country today, but back in the day, it was definitely an extra. With this addition, my days went something like this: wake up, eat breakfast, be in class by eight o'clock, get to the weight room or track before lunch, break for lunch, dash to team practice for three hours, eat dinner at the dorms, do homework, and go to bed—utterly exhausted. Repeat. After following this routine religiously week after week, people started to call me "the Hermit" because I rarely socialized and was only really seen at practice by my teammates. But I was happy because I was moving inexorably toward my goal of winning the tournament and earning that all-important wildcard.

By the time the tournament rolled around at the end of the fall season, I was in the best shape of my life and playing great tennis. And sure enough, I made it to the finals. On the day of the final, it was one of those scorching days in Palm Desert, so heat and fatigue were going to be factors in determining who prevailed in this match. Of course, the match came down to a third-set tiebreaker, both of us giving it everything we had for the all-important wildcard. I could see that my opponent was wilting as we began the tiebreaker, and it was at this point that I knew I was going to win. I had paid the price being the Hermit and doing the extra work in the weight room and on the track prior to our normal three-hour team practice. My opponent was drained, and I could have played another two sets. I won 7–6 in the third. In March of '86, I received the wildcard and ended up beating two top-twenty ranked players in the world (Greg Holmes and Peter Lundgren) to reach the round of sixteen of a major ATP tour event. I lost to Joakim Nyström from Sweden (6–3, 6–4), who went on to beat Yannick Noah in the finals and reach the highest ranking of his career at number seven in the world. And I had played him pretty close on the stadium court. My sacrifice in becoming the Hermit to accomplish a specific goal is what eventually launched me into my career six months later—my dream of becoming a professional tennis player.

Because of this defining moment in my life and the sacrifices I had to make along the way to reach these goals, my wife and I have embraced the defining moments in each of our children's lives and have taught them to make the necessary sacrifices to reach their goals. As I mentioned earlier, the sacrifices that are made will have to fit in with your family culture and values, but sacrifice is good because it teaches our children the all-important life skills that will aid them in realizing their dreams and accomplishing their goals

NOTES

1. Steve Prefontaine, in Tom Jordan *Pre: America's Greatest Running Legend, Steve Prefontaine* (Emmaus, PA: Rodale Books, 1997).

2. Robert Frost, "The Road Not Taken," Poetry Foundation, accessed March 9, 2015, http://www.poetryfoundation.org/poem/173536.

COUNT THE COST AND BECOME AN EXPERT

"There are only two options regarding commitment. You're either in or you're out. There is no such thing as life in-between."[1]

—Pat Riley

When you sit down with your children to have a goal-setting session, and when a particular goal is set, now it's time to count the cost of what it's realistically going to take to accomplish the goal before embarking on the quest (see Luke 14:28). In other words, if your child is serious about a particular goal or pursuing a dream, make sure you've done your due diligence—your research and homework—and then see if your child is still all in.

I recall a conversation with a neighbor who mentioned his son had set a very ambitious goal in a particular sport and asked me what I thought. I suggested that they sit down together and really go over all that it would take and how dedicated his son would have to be to have a realistic chance of accomplishing the goal. When we spoke about it again, he mentioned that when he had a serious discussion with his son about how dedicated he would have to be and the sacrifices he would have to make to accomplish the goal, he said his son decided that he really didn't want to set that as a goal after all. When it came down to it, he wasn't that committed. This, obviously, is much better to discover before time, money, and resources are spent starting something that won't be finished.

Don't get me wrong, I'm all for pursuing difficult things (dream big), but what I'm suggesting here is that before we start down the road of striving to reach a goal or fulfill a dream, we take stock of what it's truly going to take, the sacrifices that will have to be made, and the resources that will need to be made available to see it through to the end.

My parents became experts on how to help me and my siblings become really good tennis players. And so Cindi and I had to become experts on everything that was entailed in helping our daughters reach their goals of earning college scholarships through academics and our sons through a combination of both academics and athletics. In the tennis arena, we divided and conquered: She took on the role of being the developmental team manager, and I took on the role of coach. I reported to her—the boss.

While Cindi traveled with me my entire career and watched more tennis matches than she ever signed up for, she didn't have the background or knowledge of what it took for me to get to that level through the slog of competitive junior and collegiate tennis. If our sons were headed down this same path, she would have to become a junior tennis expert. She would have to learn about scheduling tournaments, what it took to be "endorsed" to participate in national tournaments, how to make the important team events, the ranking that was required to get into the major national events, and so on.

She asked questions, volunteered on USTA committees, and became one of the most knowledgeable tennis parents in the country. As a result, she was asked to serve on the USTA National Junior Competition Committee and was selected to be a board member for the Utah Tennis Association. Cindi's background and experience was in dance; she was a Cougarette at BYU. She learned to play tennis from my dad and is a good recreational player. She had no inherent advantage in the world of tennis, but she became an expert to help our sons reach their goals and become the best THEY could be.

In a previous chapter, I discussed using our collective skills and experience to give our children a boost. When we're not qualified or we lack the background needed to give a boost in a particular area where our children are striving to become the best THEY can be, we can do the best we can do to learn and become an expert.

The same goes for academics. Cindi and I determined when our kids were very young that academics was going to be the priority in our home. We strongly believe that the marriage of academics with athletics and the arts provides great life-lesson opportunities and can also be a pragmatic approach to paying for college through scholarships.

Even though I made a living as a professional athlete, we wanted our children to be academically inclined, so we stressed academic achievement in our home from the very beginning of our children's schooling. We set family expectations, taught our children to set goals, introduced them to the principle of alignment, and became alignment specialists.

Cindi got involved with the PTA, and we both made it a priority to be active in our kids' schools. Whenever possible, we both attended parent-teacher conferences. This let our children and the teacher know that we were committed to our children's development as students. In fact, I'm still teased by one of my all-time best recruits and players that one of his activities on his recruiting trip to BYU consisted of attending a parent-teacher conference with one of our children.

We were both profoundly impacted by a comment made by a neighbor of ours (when our children were very young) that she was in the business of raising smart children. We paid attention to this bold statement. It resonated with us because all of her children were, in fact, very smart, high-achieving students. This comment made us realize that perhaps there were things that parents could do to encourage and foster achievement in the classroom—that if one did go about achievement in the classroom in a businesslike way, even parents like us, with no *cum laude*s on our transcripts, could figure it out for our children. In time, we eventually came up with the principle of alignment and the role of parents as alignment specialists.

The point is this: In teaching your children to become the best THEY can be, if you and your spouse lack the background or experience you need to give your children a "leg up" in their chosen pursuits, then roll up your sleeves, tag team, dig in, become experts, set family expectations, affirm those expectations regularly, and become businesslike in your approach. Make achievement according to the varying abilities of your children in academics, athletics, and the arts a part of your family culture, but remember that the goal is to teach your children to become the best THEY can be, which is a different goal than raising your children to become the best.

The important thing is that we're doing everything we can to help our children realize their potential. If they end up achieving some notable things along the way, then that's a very nice bonus—"gravy," as some would say.

NOTES

1. Pat Riley, espn.com, accessed March 9, 2015, http://espn.go.com/espnw/ quote/6391571/269/there-only-two-options-regarding-commitmentin-there-no-such-thing-life-between.

CONCERTED CULTIVATION

"The major work of the world is not done by geniuses. It is done by ordinary people, with balance in their lives, who have learned to work in an extraordinary manner."[1]

—Gordon B. Hinckley

I was the product of a lot of effort from many people, starting with my parents and ending with a great wife, parents-in-law, and plenty of good coaching along the way. Like a plant, I was cultivated to accomplish what I did as a tennis player every step of the way. Remember, we're all in the business of cultivating our children.

After we had put the tenets together that formed the backbone of our family culture, we planned the work, and we're now working the plan. Cindi was active in the PTA organization, and we both got involved in issues that surrounded our children's academic pursuits. We took these things very seriously and treated them as one of the foundational pillars of our family culture—academics and pursuing excellence in the classroom.

When there were times one of our children needed help with a teacher, we listened attentively to what they perceived to be the problem or misunderstanding, and then we would coach them as to how we thought it would be best to get through it when they went back and communicated with the teacher. If necessary, we would meet with a teacher or principal as needed, along with our child. This taught them that it was okay to constructively communicate in institutional settings. Really, what we were teaching them was how to navigate the adult world, a necessary skill that requires experience. We didn't let them suffer the consequences of not knowing how to work through issues in the adult world but taught them how to do it. In academic or other adult, real-world settings, we didn't throw them in the deep end hoping they would learn how to swim, we taught them how to swim and constructively maneuver through obstacles as they presented themselves. These are all learned skills that our children must acquire either through trial and error and suffering unnecessary consequences or being taught.

To use popular terms, I would say that we operate from one end of the parent spectrum to the other—from the "Tiger Mom" to the "Helicopter Parent" to the "Hands-off Parent." We can be all of the above depending on the situation and what our child needs at the time.

After reading Malcolm Gladwell's book *Outliers: The Story of Success*, I learned that there is a term that is used to describe the point on the spectrum where Cindi and I have tried to spend most of our time as parents. That term is called *concerted cultivation*. While we don't subscribe to every facet of this term defined by sociologist Annette Lareau (some things are just not okay in our family culture when dealing with parents and authority figures), we feel there has been value in actively "fostering" and "assessing" our children's "talents, opinions and skills." [2]

As mentioned previously, we haven't ever been afraid of stepping in to save our children from themselves, believing in time that they will eventually figure things out and become ready to take on the world standing on their own two feet. Until that time, however, we are like farmers cultivating our precious "crops."

As parents, we all do the best that we can. I'm grateful that I was "cultivated" along the way and didn't have to spend too much time in the School of Hard Knocks.

NOTES

1. Gordon B. Hinckley, "Our Fading Civility," BYU commencement address, April 25, 1996, accessed March 10, 2015, http://speeches.byu.edu/index.php?act=viewitem&id=2070.

2. Malcolm Gladwell, *Outliers: The Story of Success* (New York: Little, Brown and Company, 2008), 102–104.

LIFE LESSON #14

RESILIENCE

*"The moment we believe that success is determined by
an ingrained level of ability as opposed to resilience and
hard work, we will be brittle in the face of adversity."*[1]

—Joshua Waitzkin

Certainly one of the Life Lessons learned from a career on the professional tennis tour is resilience—the ability to bounce back. Over ten years, I was the absolute winner only ten times, so that equates to winning a tournament every year. Needless to say, I had to learn how to bounce back from defeat a lot.

On the other hand, Jimmy Connors won a lot. In fact, he won more titles than any other male player in the history of the sport.[2] He is famous for saying, "I hate to lose more than I love to win."[3] I'm more of the hate-to-lose type as well. Winning was a relief, and losing was agonizing. There is nothing that bothers me more as a coach than when one of my players comes off the court in a tough loss and is all smiles. I immediately think there was no investment of heart, mind, body, and entire soul into the outcome—that prevailing in this gladiatorial test of will on the tennis court didn't mean enough. They weren't "all in" with everything they had.

I wasn't the type that I was going to go on a rampage in a loss, but I took losing very hard. Had I been a cave dweller, let's just say, I wouldn't have emerged from my cave into the sunlight for many days, probably until I reached the point of starvation. Some would say that this isn't emotionally healthy, and they would probably be right. I learned how to deal with the tragedy of losing much better as I got older because I had to: I had two little girls who needed and wanted my attention, so I couldn't be as self-absorbed, wallowing in my pity party.

The point of this Life Lesson, however, is not for me to discuss the emotional and psychological aspects of winning and losing; it's to encourage and promote the idea that teaching our children to be resilient, which is the ability to bounce back from a loss or falling short, is essential. I eventually came to find a process that I went through in defeat that would get me back to an even keel. It involved experiencing the crushing disappointment and a form of mourning followed by an objective analysis of what went wrong and what let me down and then a resolve to go back and fix whatever let me down on the practice court the next day—and so on. I admire individuals who can speed this process up and be right back, even after full investment in the outcome. I'm striving to become more like this because life's too short to dwell on mistakes or shortcomings—it's unproductive. Deal with it and move forward. Easier said than done. How I dealt with defeat is neither right nor wrong, but it worked for me. Everyone is a little different, so let me suggest that you teach and help your children to find a process that works for them that is unique to their personality.

Our children are going to have some shortcomings and bitter disappointments in their lives on the court or field, in the classroom, on stage, or in the concert hall. It's inevitable. As far as I'm concerned, it's okay for them to feel disappointment and let down for a time. But once that moment has expired, it's time to get them back up on their feet, "back in the saddle," and ready to go again.

In his book, *A Champions Mind: Lessons From a Life in Tennis,* Pete Sampras brings us inside his head and explains why losing in the final of the 1992 US Open to Stefan Edberg was the turning point in his career. He writes:

> The Edberg match was the straw that broke the camel's back. If I didn't care, who would? I had wasted two big moments, and there was no guarantee that I would experience those moments again. My future was no longer a matter of how good I could get in order to put myself in a position to win big events. I was there; I was plenty good. I wasn't developing anymore in any significant technical or physical way, I was developed (except in my grass-court game). The real question was, Did I want to win majors? The Edberg match forced me to confront that. I slowly came to a realization about myself that wasn't very pretty. . . .
>
> I went into 1993 determined never to give up in a match again.

Whatever happened, I would never lose another battle—especially a Grand Slam final or similar big opportunity—because I didn't have the heart to fight to the finish and walk off the court spent. I'd had my conversation with commitment; now it was just a matter of backing up my promise on the court."[4]

In teaching your children to become the best THEY can be, teach them that it's okay to feel disappointment when they experience the "agony of defeat," but it's not okay to dwell on it for days on end. As Zig Ziglar said, "It's not how far you fall, but how high you bounce that counts."[5] Teach them to be resilient, which is more than just not giving up or having determination. It is "the capacity to recover quickly from difficulty; toughness."[6] It is "the ability to become strong, healthy, or successful again after something bad happens."[7] When the bitterness of defeat on the court, in the classroom, or on stage stiffens their resolve to work harder to avoid those feelings in the future, then falling short has served its purpose. So be grateful for both failure and defeat.

NOTES

1. Joshua Waitzkin, interview by Scott Barry Kaufman, "Learning about Learning: an Interview with Joshua Waitzkin," January 21, 2009, http://sharpbrains.com/blog/2009/01/21/learning-about-learning-an-interview-with-joshua-waitzkin/.

2. "Jimmy Connors," Wikipedia.org, accessed March 10, 2015, http://en.wikipedia.org/wiki/Jimmy_Connors.

3. "Jimmy Connors," Electra Star Management, accessed March 10, 2015, http://jimmyconnors.net/about/.

4. Pete Sampras, *A Champion's Mind: Lessons from a Life in Tennis* (New York: Crown, 2008), 87–92.

5. Zig Ziglar, "Official Ziglar Quotes," accessed March 10, 2015, http://www.ziglar.com/quotes/its-not-how-far-you-fall.

6. Google search results, s.v. "resilience," accessed March 10, 2015, https://www.google.com/?gws_rd=ssl#q=resilience.

7. *Merriam-Webster Online*, s.v. "resilience," accessed March 10, 2015, http://www.merriam-webster.com/dictionary/resilience.

LIFE LESSON #15

WILL AND DETERMINATION

"The difference between successful people and others is not a lack of strength, not a lack of knowledge, but rather a lack in will."[1]

—Vince Lombardi

A few of my all-time favorite books and movies are *Mulan, Iron Will, Miracle, Apollo 13, The Right Stuff, Seabiscuit,* and *Green Lantern.* They are some of my favorites because they tell inspiring stories of how individuals, teams, and even horses accomplished great things through sheer willpower and determination. They say that love conquers all; I would also say that about will. If you combine the ingredients of talent and will, great things can and will be accomplished, provided it's channeled in the right direction.

Traveling to a new country every week was standard operating procedure while on the professional tennis tour, but crossing multiple time zones and oceans on long flights and playing the next day is an extreme situation, and it required a great deal of will and determination to be successful. It was these two things that helped me through some matches in two very challenging situations.

The first was in October 1986, right after I had turned pro. I had just finished playing tournaments in Tokyo and Hong Kong and was eager to be headed back home. I got a call from my agent, letting me know that he had secured a wildcard for me into the qualifying draw of the European Champions' Championship (ECC) in Antwerp, Belgium. He explained that there was significant money to be made if I won three matches and qualified for the main draw, but the catch was I had to be on a plane immediately because I would have to play the next night in Antwerp. It's a fifteen-hour-plus flight from Hong Kong to Brussels, but I was on that flight landing in Brussels the next morning, followed by a drive to Antwerp, a short practice, lunch, a light dinner, and a match that same night. For those of you who travel a lot for business, you can appreciate that this kind of an undertaking is a very tall order indeed. However, opportunity knocked. Because I had prepared my mind, my body responded, and I pulled it off and qualified. When I flew back to Utah after this tournament, I had a sizable paycheck as a reward for my willpower and determination.

The second occasion where I had to rely on willpower, determination, and "mind over matter" came in February 1990. I had committed to play a Tour event in Rio de Janeiro, Brazil. The matches, I was told, would be played on a stadium court erected on the sands of the famous Copacabana Beach. (I wish I had a photo of this unique venue because it was awesome.) Shortly after my commitment, I got a call from Tom Gorman, the Davis Cup captain, asking me if I would like to join the team that would be playing against the Czech Republic in Prague the weekend before my Brazil event. Who turns down an opportunity to be a member of the Davis Cup Team? Not me. The challenge was that I would have to fly from Prague, arrive in Rio (another fifteen-hour-plus flight) in the morning, and play that same afternoon—in the hot sun with virtually no time to adjust to the completely different playing conditions of being indoors in Prague in February and being outdoors in the southern hemisphere on the Copacabana beach the next day. Another tall order to be sure. I arrived, was picked up at the airport by a tournament driver and taken to my hotel to get something to eat, had a warm-up, played my match, and won.

While none of these stories from my career are "Ronnie Lott" cut-off-your-finger-to-play[2] kind of stories, I had other instances where will and determination helped me to win matches and my first pro tournament. In November 1989, I was playing a tournament in Bergen, Norway. It was cold. Unfortunately, I came down with a cough that turned into bronchitis, and all the cough medicine that I downed that week could not keep me from hacking away every night after playing. I ended up reaching the finals and beating a lot of good players along the way, but I never slept a wink at night. I was coughing up my lungs until sunup. To this day, I have never coughed harder, longer, and more incessantly than I did that entire week in Bergen. My whole body ached and was sore from my hacking fits. But my will and determination to get through each match that week, one day at a time, was greater than a horrible cough.

In 1990 at the French Open, I used a chair in our hotel room to climb up on the ledge of the window to try to close the curtains before I went to bed. After getting the curtains closed, I went to step down on the chair from the ledge, but the chair moved, and I came crashing down, breaking my tailbone—an unathletic move to be sure. I had Queens coming up in a couple of weeks (a major grass court warm-up tournament prior to Wimbledon), and it was doubtful that I would be ready to play because I could hardly bend, and sitting was out of the question. The thing about grass court tennis was it required a lot of volleying, which meant that every time I came to a split-step, I would have to be down low in a squat-like stance. The pain moving into that position and exploding out trying to hit a volley was intense, especially having to do it over and over again. Nevertheless, I had to find a way.

The day of my first-round match, I recall downing an absurd amount of ibuprofen. There wasn't anything else that could be done for a broken tailbone except give it time to heal, so I went out to play loaded up with enough anti-inflammatory in my system to numb a horse. It didn't help much with the pain, but I figured if I could hit a good enough first volley after coming into the net behind my serve, I had a small chance of winning, because on grass at that time points were quick with very few back-and-forth exchanges. I ended up winning 9–7 in the third and never hit better first volleys in my entire life—because I had to. Will and determination carried me through again. By the time Wimbledon came around two weeks later, I was feeling much better and ended up having the best result of my career at a Grand Slam, likely because my injury forced me to volley better than I ever had before. Other than the ATP trainer and Cindi, no one knew the pain I was playing with two weeks before. Willpower and determination can overcome big challenges and obstacles.

One summer at Lake Powell, I made the poor decision to dive off of a cliff that was way too high (unless you are from Acapulco and are a cliff diver). I entered the water a bit off, and my neck has been tweaked ever since. On occasion, I'll wake up with a horribly stiff neck that can last for weeks at a time. My first professional tournament win came in the summer of 1986 at the Berkeley Tennis club. I woke up the morning of my first round match and found that I could only turn my head to the right. Turning my head to the left was not going to happen. (I never served better in my entire life because I had to keep my service toss out to the right of me.) My neck got a little better each day, and when Jack

Kramer (yes, *the* Jack Kramer) came out onto the court after I won 6–1, 6–0 in the finals to tell me that I had only committed one unforced error the entire match (he had been doing the commentary for television), I was thinking that playing with a stiff neck wasn't so bad after all. Woody Allen understood this principle well when he said, "80 percent of success is showing up."[3] At the very minimum, teach your children to simply show up and don't beat themselves. If they are going to lose, have it be because of an opponent's superior play or performance and not because they shot themselves in the foot.

Our children have grown up in the kind of family culture that says that unless arterial blood is spurting and the bones are showing through the skin, they tough it out and get through the day.

During a recent family party, my younger sister and I were having a discussion about where this family trait came from. We discovered that it came from my mom. My dad was always compassionate about ailments, and even though my mom was tenderhearted, she wouldn't stand for any of us making excuses of any kind over a mere "flesh wound" (see *Monty Python and the Holy Grail*[4]). Cindi came from a family culture where every child could recite the following expression verbatim: "Excuses are the patches which mend the garments of failure."

With Cindi and I as products of our respective family cultures, it's no wonder that our children have some great blackmail stories in our family lore. For example, when it came to playing tennis matches with the flu, Cindi is infamous for saying to our children through the years, "That's what trash cans on the side of the court are for, use them if you have to." And they have—many times over the years.

I was so grateful that my son John—after getting an extreme case of food poisoning—grew up in this kind of a home so that he was the last player on the court with our four-year team goal of going undefeated against ITA Mountain Region opponents. He clinched the match for us 4–3 to check the box on this goal and extend our streak to 36–0. This was done even though he was able to hold down only a piece of a cookie just before going on court. I was a happy coach, a proud father, and a grateful observer to see that his will and determination were greater than the horrible episode of food poisoning.

Matthew played the first half of his high school tennis season his junior year with two ingrown toenails on his big toes, which caused him a lot of pain. When he went in to the doctor to get treatment, the doctor surgically cut out the ingrown part, telling Matthew that he would be fine in a few days. Unfortunately, infection set in, and neither toe healed properly, becoming a nasty, festering mess. We took him back to the doctor to get options. The doctor gave him two choices: Matthew could have surgery on them right then and there but would not be able to play for a month while they healed. Region and State were just around the corner, and to go back in for surgery would force him out, right when his team needed him the most. Or the doctor could write him a prescription for antibiotics, and Matthew would play through the pain but would have to be back in his office immediately following State to have his toenails completely removed and the infection scraped away. It was an easy decision for Matthew; his team needed him. Every match he played he suffered, but to his credit, he never showed it. Peeling off his blood-soaked socks after he played his last match, I had never been more proud of his no-excuse, take-one-for-the-team attitude. Matthew showed the heart of a champion and competed the best he could with a lot of class. He went on to have a terrific freshman year at BYU on the court and in the classroom and will return from his mission in July 2016. John returns in June of this year. Because of their will and determination and willingness to "cowboy up" and "take one for the team," as a father and as a coach, I can't wait to get them both back!

Will, determination, perseverance, desire, or whatever word you want to use, is essentially that characteristic that you're going to see things through—the old "when the going gets tough, the tough get going" mentality. Along with the movies mentioned above, one of my favorite stories of will and determination comes from an April 28, 2008, *Sports Illustrated* cover story that I read. It was about football Hall-of-Famer Raymond Berry, who played for the Baltimore Colts.

As the article describes, Raymond Berry was the prototypical athlete that was not blessed with natural talent but had an abundance of willpower and determination. Bowden writes about Berry in this way: "Few fans have understood that the key to victory in that game was not its celebrated coaches nor any of its marquee stars, but an ungainly wide receiver who lacked the pure athletic ability to play pros sports and whose peculiar obsessions made him and oddball to his teammates. He was, nevertheless, the prototype of the modern football player."[5]

The article goes on to reveal how Berry's desire, willpower, and work ethic helped him overcome all challenges and obstacles to become a record-setting player at his position of wide receiver and how he teamed with Johnny Unitas to win the 1958 NFL Championship against the New York Giants. One of those "obsessions" that Bowden refers to describes how Berry would spend his summers playing "an entire football game at the split end position in pantomime."[6]

> He had chosen the film of a particular game, observed each route run by the wide receiver, timed each play and interval between plays with a stopwatch and, in tiny, meticulous handwriting, sketched the patterns and noted the sequences. Every play, whether the receiver was thrown the ball or not; every huddle; every timeout; every stretch the wideout spent on the bench between offensive series. Then, consulting his handwritten script out on the grass, he acted out the game from whistle to whistle. Out on the playing field of his hometown in the dead of summer, there was no one to observe his obsessive devotion, no teammate, no neighbor, no coach. There was no one he was trying to impress. It was pure desire.[7]

Clearly, Berry was earning his "private victories" (see Covey, *Seven Habits of Highly Effective People*, 51). Raymond had this to say about will:

> After the first four years of being in the league . . . I asked myself, Where does this drive come from? I began to realize that I was doing this so differently from everybody else. I began to get very curious about the source of this drive. It was a powerful thing. I began to realize it was a tremendous gift. It had everything to do with how I was playing, and it just did not get deterred by obstacles. I finally realized God gave me that drive. It was just as much a part of me as speed, jumping ability, strength, weight. The desire and the drive were more important than all of them. They made me.[8]

All of us have within ourselves the ability to reach our true potential as human beings and to achieve in those areas where we have some natural talent, will, desire, and determination. As parents, we can help our children to become the best THEY can be by exposing them to books, movies, stories, and articles (like this one about Raymond Berry) that will inspire them to strive to accomplish their goals. Teach them to never underestimate the power of will and determination as they strive to slay their personal dragons.

One of my favorite poems is one you've probably heard: "Stick to your task 'til it sticks to you; beginners are many, but enders are few. Honor, power, place, and praise will always come to the one who stays. Stick to your task 'til it sticks to you; bend at it, sweat at it, smile at it too; for out of the bend and the sweat and the smile will come life's victories after a while."[9]

As we teach our children to become the best THEY can be, it often comes down to simply encouraging them to tough things out, roll with the punches, and practice good old-fashioned stick-to-itiveness. Talent is a great thing, but will and determination reign supreme in my book.

NOTES

1. Vince Lombardi, quoted in The Biography.com, "Vince Lombardi," A&E Television Networks, accessed March 10, 2015, http://www.biography.com/people/vince-lombardi-9385362#final-years.

2. "Ronnie Lott's Amputated Pinkie Finger" MMQB: NFL 95, June 17, 2014, http://mmqb.si.com/2014/06/17/nfl-history-in-95-objects-ronnie-lott-amputated-pinkie-finger/.

3. Woody Allen, interview by Steve Weintraub, "Woody Allen Interview—Vicky Cristina Barcelona," *Collider*, August 15, 2008, http://collider.com/woody-allen-interview-vicky-cristina-barcelona/.

4. *Monty Python and the Holy Grail*, directed by Terry Gilliam and Terry Jones (UK: EMI Films, 1975).

5. Mark Bowden, "The Best Game Ever, Colts vs. Giants (1958): How John Unitas and Raymond Berry Invented the Modern NFL," *Sports Illustrated*, April 28, 2008.

6. Ibid., 66.

7. Ibid., 66.

8. Ibid., 77.

9. Author unknown, quoted in Thomas S. Monson "Finishers Wanted," June 1989, https://www.lds.org/ensign/1989/06/finishers-wanted?lang=eng.

DISCIPLINE

"In reading the lives of great men, I found that the first victory they won was over themselves. . . . Self-discipline with all of them came first."

—Attributed to Harry S. Truman

One of the most important books that was given to me when I was young came from my mother, who passed away after a five-year bout with cancer a month after I was married in May 1987. This book has become one of my treasured possessions because it came from her. It's called *The Disciplined Life: Studies in the Fine Art of Christian Discipleship* by Richard Shelley Taylor.

The first line in the first chapter begins with this: "The world belongs to the disciplined."[1] As a parent and a coach of many young men through the years, I have seen this firsthand. I've had players through the years with mediocre talent accomplish great things and become the best they could be on the tennis court and in the classroom simply because they had great discipline. They were willing to do the really hard stuff—the stuff that required a lot of discipline on a day-to-day basis. Having been a student athlete myself, I know firsthand that the life can be monotonous: Wake up early for strength and conditioning, go to classes, eat lunch, and practice for up to three hours, eat dinner, do homework, and go to bed. Repeat over and over through days, weeks, months, and years. There are, of course, some incredible highs that are experienced during these years because of the exhilaration of competition and the satisfying aspects and camaraderie that go along with being a part of team, but for the most part, being a student athlete is a lot of hard work and takes a lot of discipline. It's "mind over mattress," as Stephen R. Covey would say.[2]

I have always liked how Taylor defined self-discipline. "In a general sense, self-discipline is the ability to regulate conduct by principle and judgment rather than impulse, desire, high pressure, or social custom. It is basically the ability to subordinate."[3] My response to my players through the years when they tell me they don't feel like doing something has been to paraphrase a line from Taylor when he wrote, "'Young man, has it ever occurred to you that most of the world's work is done by people who 'don't feel like it'?"[4] The ability to subordinate what might feel good right now to a long-term goal that will provide substantive satisfaction for a lifetime is a skill or attribute that I believe can be taught and learned.

I have seen some great examples of discipline with my own children. When John and Matthew were young, they decided that they wanted to get good enough to earn tennis scholarships to a major Division I university, which is a lofty goal. This goal would require them to devote thousands and thousands of hours of deliberate practice to reach this high level of mastery. Since they couldn't get a lot of practice done in the afternoons because of limited tennis court time, they decided they needed to get their work done in the mornings before school. Because I was their sole coach, this involved me and very early mornings, something I was happy to do if they were committed. The entire time throughout their elementary, junior high, and high school years, I never had to wake them up. In fact, many times they would come into my room to wake me up. They had learned to subordinate how they felt getting up in the early-morning hours, especially during the winter months when it was so cold, to their long-term goals. They, along with Jordan and Tara, also learned how to study diligently and for long hours at a time on a consistent basis and subordinate more fun things to their academic goals. I'm pleased that both Josh and Halle, our two youngest, are following in their older siblings' footsteps and are pursuing their own goals on the court and in the classroom.

Taylor had this to say about discipline:

> Many a young person would like to become a doctor or a top-flight scientist but never will, simply because he will not buckle down to the demanding years of hard study. Many young people would like to achieve artistry and mastery in music but they never will, simply because they will not face the long hours of monotonous practice year after year. They may through natural talent become singers or pianists of a sort, but they will not pay that extra price for true excellence. They

are too lazy and self-indulgent to pommel themselves to the top. Their ambitions may not be beyond their capacity, but they are beyond their discipline. The world is full of naturally brilliant people who never rise above mediocrity because they will not make the sacrifice which superiority requires.[5]

I'll never forget an expression my dad would say when it came to getting to bed at night, getting up in the mornings, and being productive: "It's hard to soar with the eagles when you're up all night with the owls." In teaching our children to become the best THEY can be, focus on discipline. Discipline goes hand-in-hand with goal setting and an achievement mentality that can be instilled in our children. Sit down with your children and help them set THEIR goals, and then get them started practicing the kind of discipline it's going to take to accomplish those goals. Become an alignment specialist. Take courage and have patience. You're not going to be able to give them one speech one time about discipline. It hasn't worked in my role as a tennis coach in getting my players to be more disciplined in their shot-selection while playing critical matches, and it hasn't worked in my role as a father with my children. At times, it will be like the siege described in getting them to live by the principle of alignment.

In our family, we've found that it takes constant teaching, modeling, inspiring, and training on our part to foster and cultivate disciplined decision making and living in our children, but of all the things that are worth time and energy as parents, it can certainly be argued that instilling discipline is one of the most important.

NOTES

1. Richard Shelley Taylor, *The Disciplined Life* (Minneapolis, MN: Beacon Hill, 1962), 17.

2. Stephen R. Covey, *Principle-Centered Leadership* (New York: Fireside, 1991), 49.

3. Richard Shelley Taylor, *The Disciplined Life*, 27.

4. Ibid., 34.

5. Ibid., 23.

LIFE LESSON #17

IF

*"No misfortune is so bad that whining
about it won't make it worse."*[1]

—Jeffrey R. Holland

Through wins and losses over the years, I've learned an important life lesson that I've tried to pass onto my children: Sometimes we may set the right goals and be perfectly aligned in our habits and work ethic to give ourselves a realistic chance to achieve the goal but find in the end, it may not be in the cards for us. This is when we take comfort in Rudyard Kipling's epic poem "If—."

During the summer of 1986, I played a pro tournament at the Yale University tennis facility in New Haven, Connecticut. As I was roaming through the indoor facility, I happened upon the poem "If—" pinned up on the wall. It was the first time I had been acquainted with this timeless poem and was inspired by its message, so I pulled it down and found someone in the building who could make a copy for me. I still have this same treasured copy in my files. If you're not familiar with this poem, let me share it with you:

> *If you can keep your head when all about you*
> *Are losing theirs and blaming it on you,*
> *If you can trust yourself when all men doubt you,*
> *But make allowance for their doubting too;*
> *If you can wait and not be tired by waiting,*
> *Or being lied about, don't deal in lies,*
> *Or being hated, don't give way to hating,*
> *And yet don't look too good, nor talk too wise:*

If you can dream—and not make dreams your master;
If you can think—and not make thoughts your aim;
If you can meet with Triumph and Disaster
And treat those two impostors just the same;
If you can bear to hear the truth you've spoken
Twisted by knaves to make a trap for fools,
Or watch the things you gave your life to, broken,
And stoop and build 'em up with worn-out tools:

If you can make one heap of all your winnings
And risk it on one turn of pitch-and-toss,
And lose, and start again at your beginnings
And never breathe a word about your loss;
If you can force your heart and nerve and sinew
To serve your turn long after they are gone,
And so hold on when there is nothing in you
Except the Will which says to them: "Hold on!"

If you can talk with crowds and keep your virtue,
Or walk with Kings—nor lose the common touch,
If neither foes nor loving friends can hurt you,
If all men count with you, but none too much;
If you can fill the unforgiving minute
With sixty seconds' worth of distance run,
Yours is the Earth and everything that's in it,
And—which is more—you'll be a Man, my son.[2]

I ended up winning both the singles and doubles events at this pro tournament, so on top of becoming familiar with this masterpiece of a poem, I was moving in the right direction toward my goal of becoming one of the top seventy-five players in the world while still an amateur. Fast-forward to the moment on July 4, 1990, when I'm about to take Centre Court at Wimbledon to play Lendl. Since this was my first time playing on Centre Court, not only in the quarterfinals but also on prime-time TV in front of a worldwide viewing audience, needless to say, I was nervous. I was anxious to get out on the court and start warming up, knowing that would help me to relax and release some tension. But, of course, being Wimbledon, there is a strict protocol for how things are done.

There's a little anteroom that they use to hold the players before they step out onto the pristine grass of Centre Court. As Lendl and I were both waiting to get the signal to take the court, someone was telling us that there was royalty in the box and going over the correct protocol—a turn and a bow—that was supposed to be performed as we walked by the Royal Box. Honestly, I really had no idea what I was supposed to do, having never played on Centre Court before. And with so many other things on my mind, I wasn't really paying attention, so this just added to the stress of the moment.

We received the signal to take the court, and there it was, stenciled just above the door that you have to duck through to step onto the iconic grass of Centre Court at Wimbledon: "If you can meet with triumph and disaster and treat those two imposters the same." This gave me a big smile and helped me to relax. Not only did I feel like a Renaissance man that I actually knew where this line came from, but it was also a reminder of what an incredible opportunity I had in front of me, win or lose, triumph or disaster, it was an experience of a lifetime. And I will forever be grateful to Ivan for his sensitivity. As we were nearing the Royal Box, walking side by side along the baseline, he whispered to me, "Just do what I do, and you'll be fine." I did exactly what he suggested. Disaster avoided. I'm glad to say that I didn't become the first player to botch up the bow to the Royal Box on Centre Court.

This poem has been analyzed by brilliant scholars the world over, but to me one of the central messages of "If—" is to not lose perspective through the "triumphs and disasters" and the normal vicissitudes of life. I had my life planned out: number one junior ranking, then to UCLA where I would become an all-American, and finally to the pros where I would win Wimbledon and other Grand Slams, become a rich and famous tennis player, and retire to Hawaii to live out the rest of my life hanging out on the beach. I was banking on what Pancho Segura, a tennis legend, told me when my dad and I played him and his son in a national father-and-son doubles tournament—that I would become a household name.

While I had significant wins over some of the best players in the world and enjoyed a successful professional career, I didn't win Wimbledon or other Grand Slams, and I'm not currently retired and hanging out on a beach in Hawaii. To this day, I believe I was capable of accomplishing my dream of winning Wimbledon, but the timing of my mother's life-ending bout with cancer, which kept my father, who was my coach and mentor, from being with me out on the tour when I had just turned pro, and other factors, proved to be daunting. In fact, after retirement in 1995 largely due to a nagging elbow injury, I felt I still had it in me, but it was time for me to move on.

When I accepted the Professional Tennis Registry's National Collegiate Coach of the Year award in 2010, I was someone who had won some and lost some but had learned to "treat those two impostors the same."

In teaching your children to become the best THEY can be, teach them that their lifelong goals and dreams may or may not be realized, that their best-laid plans and the most ardent effort over many years is no guarantee that every goal of theirs will be accomplished. But if they fill their lives, thinking rationally but heeding their heart, working hard toward fulfilling dreams and enjoying the ride, and never relinquishing those dreams, then they've figured out what life is really all about—learning and growing from our experiences. If our children can become the kind of people that Kipling describes, then they will truly inherit the "earth and everything that's in it."

NOTES

1. Jeffrey R. Holland, "The Tongue of Angels," April 2007, https://www.lds.org/general-conference/2007/04/the-tongue-of-angels?lang=eng.

2. Rudyard Kipling, "If—" Poetry Foundation, accessed March 10, 2015, http://www.poetryfoundation.org/poem/175772.

LIFE LESSON #18

THE POWER WITHIN

"What lies behind us and what lies before us are tiny matters compared to what lies within us."[1]

—Henry S. Haskins

There are some great benefits and challenges in pursuing the sport of tennis. The benefit is that it is an individual sport, so winning is all up to you. The challenge is that tennis is an individual sport, so losing is all up to you as well; you don't have teammates to rely on when you're having a bad day. These are the days that you must rely on the power within. And likewise, in teaching your children to become the best THEY can be, teach them how to tap into the power within.

One of my favorite movie scenes comes from a film called *Willow*. Willow Ufgood, a dwarf, has a desire to be a great magician and apprentice with the High Aldwin to further develop his magical talents. As a test to see who will be his apprentice, the High Aldwin holds out his hand and asks the hopefuls which finger holds the power to control the world. Willow's initial instinct is to look to his own finger but brushes that thought aside and ends up choosing one of the Master's, which, of course, is the wrong answer. The right answer was his own all along and is exactly what the High Aldwin wanted to see Willow conclude for himself.[2]

As author Stephen R. Covey has said, "If you start to think the problem is 'out there', stop yourself. That thought is the problem."[3] Having grown up with the Coveys and spent a lot of time with them, I picked up on an expression that was used pervasively in the Covey culture. It's called *R & I*, which means that you need to use your "resourcefulness and initiative." That stuck with me through the years, and so when it came time to raise our own children, Cindi and I incorporated this expression as we've tried to teach our children to be independent-minded and to tap into the power within before looking for solutions outside of themselves. I've also taught members of my tennis team this important principle through the years.

One of our most comedic R & I stories comes from one of our annual summer trips to Lake Powell with Cindi's family. On the morning of day one at Lake Powell, the goal is always to find the best campsite on the lake. To me, it's just another competition against the other new arrivals who are also striving for the same goal. There is no room for an abundance mentality because there is a scarcity of beach space. This is a zero-sum game with definite winners and losers (see *Seven Habits of Highly Effective People,* 219).

One year, I was given the assignment to go out in the lead boat to scout out and secure a nice beach that would serve as a suitable campsite for the week. To aid in this important mission, I was also given the resources of two jet skis, with my daughter Tara on one and my son John on the other. We had been out for quite some time and were unsuccessful, so I was starting to get anxious. I was failing in this all-important assignment, but as John would say, "I was not trying to lose this match." We started down a canyon with John and Tara right behind me when the kids from the back of the boat started yelling that John and Tara had stopped and were signaling that something was wrong. (It turned out that Tara's jet ski had some mechanical issues and quit.) Of course, I couldn't go back and help them; they could fend for themselves. I was like Gene Kranz in Mission Control for the Apollo 13 mission, and failure was not an option. I had to find a campsite.

A few hours later, we all met up in the middle of the lake. I had failed. Someone else in our group had found a mediocre campsite, but it would have to do. It was getting late, and we needed to get the big houseboat secured and anchored for the night. Cindi then asked where John and Tara were, and I was ratted out by the kids in my boat who were more than eager to spill the beans that I had left them down some canyon. I couldn't remember where I had left them, and they had no radio, so there was no way we could contact them. To say I was in trouble would be a huge understatement—like saying the Titanic sprung a leak; I was in a whirlwind of wrath, and there was no shelter from this storm. Search parties were sent out in the direction that I had come from. An hour later, which seemed like an eternity, we received a radio call from a houseboat that said they had Tara and John onboard and they were safe. They told us where they were located, so we sent out my brother-in-law to get them. When he boarded the boat, he reported back to us that John and Tara were just sitting down to enjoy a nice steak dinner as if they were part of the family. They were calm, relaxed, and quite pleased with themselves, telling him they had used their R & I to tie the jet skis together and used the working one to tow the other until they found a houseboat to call us from. Meanwhile, I was trying to stay afloat in "tsunami-like" conditions. All I can say is, "Thank heavens they were safe," as much for my sake as theirs.

Similar to finding safe harbor with a broken-down jet ski using R & I, a tennis match is typically not won or lost on talent alone, but rather rests on a player's capacity to make necessary adjustments, be resilient, and maintain mental and emotional equilibrium from start to finish. It really comes down to being resourceful in coming up with strategies during the course of a match to counter an opponent's initiatives and to advance your own. Tennis has often been compared to the game of chess, with a distinctive opening, middle, and endgame.

And so it is in the classroom or on the field, court, track, stage, or hall that our children are taught to be resourceful. Here they learn to use their initiative and understand that they themselves are perfectly capable of coming up with the correct solutions to align themselves and advance in positive ways toward their goals.

In other words, teach your children that the finger that holds the power to control the world is their own and that this is the power that each of them holds within—the ability to create their own destinies.

I was fortunate to have read a book by authors Bristol and Sherman when I was a teenager. They had this to say on the subject:

> All the great, successful men and women in this world have made use of this idea. It has been the dominant idea in their lives. Without it they could never have been great, in their way, or successful. What *is* this idea? It is the realization that *what you picture in your mind, if you picture it clearly and confidently and persistently enough, will eventually come to pass in your life!* That's it! Oh, of course, there's a little more to it than that. But boiled down to the very essence, the wise men said it all when they said: "As a Man thinketh in his mind and in his heart so is he!"[4]

In teaching your children to become the best THEY can be, teach them that they have within them a God-given power to determine right from wrong and be solution-minded beings with the ability to picture in their mind's eye the outcomes they want to make realities. And teach them to use their R & I.

NOTES

1. Henry S. Haskins in "Meditations in Wall Street," (New York: William Morrow & Co., 1940).

2. George Lucas and Bob Dolman, *Willow*, directed by Ron Howard (San Francisco: Lucasfilm, 1988).

3. Stephen R. Covey, *The Seven Habits of Highly Effective People: Powerful Lessons in Personal Change* (New York: Free Press, 2004), 93.

4. Claude M. Bristol and Harold Sherman, *TNT The Power Within You: How to Release the Forces Inside You & Get What You Want!* (New York: Fireside, 1992), 25.

LIFE LESSON #19

LINE UPON LINE

"Twenty years from now you will be more disappointed by the things that you didn't do than by the ones you did do. So throw off the bowlines. Sail away from the safe harbor. Catch the trade winds in your sails. Explore. Dream. Discover."[1]

—H. Jackson Brown Jr.

After turning pro following the US Open in September, I set my sights on my next goal—to reach the top ten. My dad was concerned about my approach. His coaching advice was to focus on becoming a top seventy-five player in the world, and then work on fifty, twenty-five, fifteen, ten, and so on up to one. He was right.

In teaching your children to be the best THEY can be, teach them the law of the harvest: we reap what we sow (see Galatians 6:7) and that the process of growth and sustainable success typically follows a continuum of "line upon line" and "precept upon precept" (see Isaiah 28:10). In other words, we don't move from being a top one hundred player in the world to number one without a lot of intermediary steps along the way. This principle can be applied to our efforts in the classroom as well as in our activities in music and the arts. For example, we don't start out as the first-chair violinist without paying our dues along the way first. Teach them that becoming the best THEY can be has its own timeline, and that they should set their goals and stay focused on the daily processes that will help them realistically align with their desired objectives without trying to force it. Success will come in its own due time.

NOTES

1. H. Jackson Brown Jr., *P.S. I Love You* (Nashville, TN: Rutledge Hill, 1990).

VALUE EDUCATION

"The true sign of intelligence is not knowledge but imagination."

—Unknown

During the ten years I spent traveling the world on the Tour, I received a broad, informal education. I learned enough words in Russian, Japanese, and Italian to greet people, say please and thank you, and enough French and Spanish to exchange greetings, ask for directions, and order food at a restaurant—the basics. I'm grateful that my job allowed me to see the world, experience different languages and cultures, and learn from all of these experiences.

The fact of the matter is that even though I came from a home that valued formal education, and my father was a college professor, going to college for me was supposed to have been a one-year plan: I wanted to be like John McEnroe and Jimmy Connors, who both went to college for a year (Stanford and UCLA respectively), won the NCAA Championships as freshmen, and turned pro. This was my goal. I ended up turning pro after my sophomore year, and even though I didn't win the NCAA Championships, I felt I was ready after I had reached a ranking of top one hundred in the world and had significant wins over some of the best players in the world at the time. I made my decision regarding foregoing my formal education at UCLA and never looked back. I dreamed about being a pro tennis player my entire life and felt it was my time to make the jump and seize the day—to strike while the iron was hot.

But one thing is certain: I came to value a formal education, and that's why we've stressed that pathway in our home with all of our children. In

1992, with Jordan and Tara nearing school age, I realized that the end of my playing career was in sight. I was only twenty-six years old, so I knew I would have a long working life in front of me. I also knew that a bachelor's degree would open up doors that would otherwise be closed in the working world. Where I have been for the last fifteen years, for example—a coach at BYU—would not have been possible without a bachelor's degree. So I transferred a year's worth of my UCLA credits to BYU.

For the next three years, when Team Pearce (me, Cindi, Jordan, Tara, and John in 1994) left our home to go out on Tour, we traveled with suitcases for each of us, an equipment bag, a two-person stroller and diaper bag, and an entire duffel bag filled with textbooks. Can you picture us traipsing through an airport? What's even more comical is that for some reason, I had an aversion to paying porter's fees, so I insisted on carrying all of these bags by myself.

A side note example of the ridiculousness of my cheapness is when we settled in to the Earls Court area for a month in London for the warm-up grass court tournaments. Because I was a creature of habit, my favorite restaurants were in this area, and we had easy access by Tube into the center of the city and out to Wimbledon. All Grand Slam tournaments are played over two weeks. One thing that we enjoyed at Wimbledon is that they didn't schedule matches on the middle Sunday, which allowed us to go to Church services at the Hyde Park ward. I hated to spend money on taxis, so we always traveled underground. Cindi and I would struggle through two different Tube lines, dragging our kids, a stroller, and a diaper bag to go to Church. By the time we got there an hour later, we were all in a sweat and frazzled. With John's arrival, Cindi "gently refused" to ride the Tube for these outings.

At the end of my career, when I became less cheap and also started to pay porters to carry our bags, we splurged on a taxi to go to Church one Sunday. We piled into the taxi outside of our flat in Earls Court, drove a few hundred yards up one street, turned, and drove a few hundred yards down another and arrived at the meetinghouse in a couple of minutes. We could have walked there in ten minutes. We still get a good laugh out of our street-level geographical shortcomings, my cheapness, and Cindi's gentle persuasion.

After two years of carrying a bag full of textbooks around the world and another four years after my retirement from the Tour in 1995, along with years of correspondence with professors on papers, assignments, and exams, and weeks on campus attending seminars, I became a college graduate in August 1999. To this day, it is one of the most significant days of my life—a day I will never forget. Thomas Paine said it best when he wrote, "What we obtain too cheap, we esteem too lightly: it is dearness only that gives every thing its value."[1] Jordan and Tara were old enough to remember my graduation and how important this day was to me. I believe this inculcated a profound sense of the importance and value of pursuing a formal education, and I'm grateful that they have been such good examples to the rest of our children.

Needless to say, a formal education became very dear to me. With two years at UCLA and seven years in BYU's program, it took me nine years to complete my bachelor's degree. When I think about the number of years it took me to graduate, it reminds me of the scene from the movie *Tommy Boy* when Tommy says, "You know, a lot of people go to college for seven years." Richard responds by saying, "Yeah, they're called doctors."[2]

Well, I'm not a doctor, but I learned to value a formal education and the opportunity it has provided me to work at an incredible institution like BYU. An informal education through travel, experiencing other cultures, and reading out of the best books and literature is also a major part of lifelong learning. I'm grateful that tennis provided me with a formal and informal education, so let me give you my "educated" opinion: if you're ever staying in Earls Court, walk to the Hyde Park Chapel, and don't take the Tube!

NOTES

1. Thomas Paine, *The American Crisis*, no. 1, December 23, 1776, accessed March 10, 2015, http://www.gutenberg.org/files/3741/3741-h/3741-h.htm#link2H_4_0005.

2. *Tommy Boy*, directed by Peter Segal (Hollywood, CA: Paramount Pictures, 1995).

LIFE LESSON #21

THE FUNDAMENTALS

"It starts with complete command of the fundamentals."[1]

—Jesse Owens

I was fortunate to have a father, whom I refer to as Master Splinter (the mentor of the *Teenage Mutant Ninja Turtles*) because he is one of the best all-time teachers of the fundamentals of tennis. Because of his attention to detail and mastery of stroke production, I, as well as all of my siblings, became accomplished tennis players. Most important, he taught us all how important it was to get it right from the very beginning.

My dad, and the emphasis he put on getting the technique right from the very beginning, would wholeheartedly agree with this statement from Michael Jordan: "You can practice shooting eight hours a day, but if your technique is wrong, then all you become is good at shooting the wrong way. Get the fundamentals down and the level of everything you do will rise."[2]

This principle is the cornerstone of long-term, sustainable success in all endeavors, whether it be in the classroom, concert hall, arena, or on the court, field, or stage. Some look for the best teachers at the end of their child's development. I would suggest the exact opposite: get your children involved with the best teachers and instructors at the beginning of their development—if you're serious. If you wait for the best to put the "icing on the cake," you may never get a cake to put the icing on.

Some of the best teachers have been fathers and mothers who have worked with their own children. Let me name a few in the sport of tennis: Jimmy Evert, the father of Chris Evert; Richard Williams, the father of

Venus and Serena Williams; Gloria Connors, the mother of Jimmy Connors; and Wayne Bryan, the father of Bob and Mike Bryan. Parents wear many different hats while raising their children and are often the best teachers because they are so invested in their child's progress and development. So don't be afraid to be your child's coach or teacher, but get the fundamentals right from the beginning.

NOTES

1. Jesse Owens, quoted in Mike Riley "4 Quotes from the sports world to inspire PR pros," PR Daily, June 25, 2012, http://www.prdaily.com/Main/Articles/4_quotes_from_the_sports_world_to_inspire_PR_pros_11993.aspx.

2. Michael Jordan, quoted in Nick Scheidies "How to Be Like Mike: 21 Life Lessons from Michael Jordan," accessed March 10, 2015, http://www.incomediary.com/how-to-be-like-mike-20-life-lessons-from-michael-jordan.

MENTAL TOUGHNESS AND BECOMING A GREAT COMPETITOR

"Every quarterback can throw a ball; every running back can run; every receiver is fast; but that mental toughness that you talk about translates into competitiveness."[1]

—Tom Brady

Teach your children to be mentally tough and to become great competitors. Before moving on, let me clarify my first sentence: becoming mentally tough and a great competitor does not necessarily mean that our children will inevitably become great champions; it simply means that we teach them to prepare, be resilient and resourceful, stay present minded, and endure to the end, no matter how agonizing competition can be at times. I'm sure there are much more precise definitions out there as to what "mental toughness" and being a "great competitor" really mean, but essentially that's what these words mean to me. To this day, I'm still learning about what goes into being considered mentally tough and a great competitor, but one thing I do believe very strongly is that great competitors aren't born but are made—becoming a great competitor is a learned skill.

One important lesson I learned from my tennis career is being satisfied with myself—win or lose—if in my heart of hearts I knew that I had absolutely given everything I had to the effort and that I held nothing back. When I hit an outright return winner on Lendl's second serve on set point to clinch the third set, I crossed the threshold of being satisfied with my performance. From that point on, I was in it for the win and knew I was now capable of winning that match, even though I was still down two sets to one. Unfortunately, it didn't come about, but I came away knowing that I had given it my best and felt good about my performance.

On another occasion, I was playing a doubles match at the Kremlin Cup in Moscow, Russia. Since this tournament had a small draw and a lot of prize money, winning even one round was significant. By the luck of the draw, my partner and I had a very winnable first-round match. We won the first set and had many chances to put the match away in the second set, but both of us kept choking. I was literally—not figuratively—about to pull my hair out because I was so frustrated with myself. Finally, we got to a tie-breaker, with me serving 5–2, which is almost a sure win. While still a painful memory, I gagged again and again to give away the second set. By this time I was like a raving lunatic on the court, and as a result, our chances were going down the tubes of having any chance of winning the third set.

Fortunately, during the break between the second and third set, I came to the realization that I was being my own worst enemy on the court and that my frustration with myself was only contributing to self-defeating behavior. I had let the pressure of the moment get to me. I reasoned with myself and came to the conclusion that the only thing I had control over was staying focused on one point at a time and being process-oriented, never looking back at past mistakes or looking forward to potential outcomes—positive or negative—and simply committing to do the best that I could. Almost a cliché, "do the best you can, and that's all you can do" was my conclusion to giving myself the best possible chance of winning this match, so it's stuck with me.

Pressure, if not channeled properly, can bring out the worst in us instead of the best. Finding relief from the pressure I was feeling by recognizing—and bringing to the forefront of my mind—that all I could do was my absolute best to try my hardest and stay focused on the present (each and every point, one point at a time) helped my partner and I to a non-emotional and comfortable third-set win, 6–3.

I've never forgotten the principles that I learned from this match about being mentally tough and competing:

1. Prepare as best you can for success.

2. Focus on the process and the present, not the outcomes (one point at a time).

3. Recognize that humans aren't infallible; we all make mistakes, so accept it.

4. If your motives are pure, do the best you can, and that's all you can do.

Dr. Allen Fox, a former Bruin tennis great, a fellow quarterfinalist at Wimbledon, and a friend of mine, gives a great explanation about how our natural "escapist" mentality takes over when the pressure is really on and how we can combat it. The problem of counteracting our natural defense mechanism isn't one of a lack of information, he suggests; it's a lack of motivation.

> *The problem is getting them to do something about it.* This is ultimately a matter of convincing players to use the intelligent parts of their brains to override their counterproductive, albeit normal, escapist emotional parts. The lower functions of the brain, embodied in the emotional system, don't give a hoot about winning tennis matches. They just want to reduce the stress right now. [author's note—this is me at the Kremlin Cup.] They want "out" and are in no mood to negotiate. The higher functions—the rational, intelligent parts—understand long-term goals (like winning tennis matches) and must simply overpower them. This is difficult because these emotions are so insistent. Giving up their escapist defenses requires constant conscious vigilance because the urges are always there, just below the surface, and ready to pounce. If the players lose confidence, get mentally tired, or become more stressed than usual they are likely to slacken their resolve, and out will pop the defenses.[2]

Mental toughness and awareness are skills that help us to be successful on the court, in the classroom, and in all other areas of our lives. My father always taught me that you're not competing against your opponent but yourself, and the essence of competition is learning how to control your emotions and will your body to do what the mind is telling it to do; it's really about self-control and discipline.

Having a positive attitude, of course, is much better than having a negative one, but people sometimes become confused when their positive attitude and energy don't always translate into victory on the court or field or in the classroom. Fox has a great answer to this conundrum:

> During tennis competition, as with the other sports, positive emotions help but do not *guarantee* good play. This fact tends to confuse players, because they often find that they still lose even after disciplining their emotions positively and well. So they start to think emotional control has no value. And they are dead wrong! Even though good emotions do not guarantee a victory, bad emotions usually guarantee a loss. Emotions only set the stage for quality of play that follows, but

they don't control it. Good emotions only make good play *more likely;* they guarantee nothing.[3]

Opposition is necessary for our children to grow and develop because it allows them opportunities to focus their energies, talents, mights, minds, and wills on a specific goal. I was taught to embrace competition.

Tennis icon Billy Jean King learned how to embrace competition and big-pressure moments when she faced Bobby Riggs in a cultural phenomenon of the seventies known as the "Battle of the Sexes" tennis match. To get through the pressures she faced to defeat Riggs, she came up with a philosophy of treating pressure as a privilege.

> At first, I felt obligated to play Riggs, but I chose to embrace as a privilege the pressure that threatened to overwhelm me. This changed my entire mindset and allowed me to deal with the situation more calmly. And as time went on I began to see the match as something I *got* to do instead of something I *had* to do. . . . Sometimes pressure will take you out of your comfort zone, and not many people like that feeling—after all, it is called a "comfort zone" for a reason! You might not believe it, but because pressure is a motivator, and going outside of the zone can be a very good thing. Embracing new opportunities is truly the best way to see how far you can go, and that leads to growth—not to mention fun! And what is life without growth and fun?[4]

Sometimes we get afraid of big moments—an important test, a big match or game, a concert or performance in front of a large crowd, speaking in Church, or teaching Gospel Doctrine class in Sunday School. At times like these, I like to reflect on one of my favorite works, which tells us that we've already passed the test—win or lose—by simply being in the "arena" of competition in the first place. It is Roosevelt's "The Man in the Arena":

> It is not the critic who counts; not the man who points out how the strong man stumbles, or where the doer of deeds could have done them better. The credit belongs to the man who is actually in the arena, whose face is marred by dust and sweat and blood; who strives valiantly; who errs, who comes short again and again, because there is no effort without error and shortcoming; but who does actually strive to do the deeds; who knows great enthusiasms, the great devotions; who spends himself in a worthy cause; who at the best knows in the end the triumph of high achievement, and who at the worst, if he fails, at least fails while daring greatly, so that his place shall never be with those cold and timid souls who neither know victory nor defeat.[5]

Many are also familiar with Michael Jordan's quote, "I've missed more than 9,000 shots in my career. I have lost almost 300 games. [On] 26 occasions I have been entrusted to take the game winning shot and missed. I have failed over and over and over again in my life. And that is why I succeed."[6] Great competitors like Michael Jordan believe in themselves even when they've failed in the past. Great competitors are resilient; they bounce back from defeat.

After the match against Lendl, I came back into the locker room, and Jimmy Connors, one of the greatest competitors of all time, came over to congratulate me on my performance and to tell me that in the future I needed to be more aware of the body language of my opponent. He told me that Lendl was obviously feeling the pressure and was nervous about going into a fifth set as it got to 4–4 in the fourth. He told me that I was so focused on myself that I neglected to get a feel for my opponent, which could have given me an extra boost at that critical time to seize the opportunity. I've never forgotten that sage advice, and now as a college coach, I always teach my guys to pay attention to their opponents to try to get a feel for their stress levels at critical times and seize the opportunity when they are vulnerable. Above all else, though, is the power of will and desire, along with the ability to focus and maintain a high intensity level for as long as it takes to complete a match. That, in my view, is what makes champions.

Another aspect of becoming a great competitor is mental toughness, which can also be applied to any endeavor. Mentally tough competitors stay focused on the present. They aren't worried about something that's already happened, a mistake that was made, or a note that was missed, nor are they thinking about what may happen in the future. Instead, they stay focused and are totally immersed—body, mind, and spirit—in the present. As Master Oogway teaches Po in the movie *Kung Fu Panda,* "Yesterday is history, tomorrow is a mystery, but today is a gift. That is why they call it the present."[7] This is an important skill to master: staying present-minded.

When I reached the quarterfinals of Wimbledon in 1990, I didn't even look at the draw ahead of who I was playing the next day. In other words, I wasn't worried about playing Lendl on day one of the tournament because I was solely focused on Ronnie Båthman, who I played in the first round, and so on. I followed this formula with exactness through to playing Lendl in the quarters, and this served me well throughout my career.

I've met with Billy Jean a few times during my career, and I am proud that I was a member of the New Jersey Stars, the World Team Tennis Champions (the tennis league she founded) of 1995 while a teammate of tennis legend, Martina Navratilova. Her concept—that pressure is a privilege and not a burden—has helped me to look at aspects of mental toughness and competitiveness in transformational ways, which has helped me as a parent and as a coach.

Perhaps some of our children will become what the world would deem as "champions," but that is not the goal. The goal is to teach them to be mentally tough (resilient, resourceful, undaunted, persistent, positive, and disciplined) and to compete—to absolutely know within their heart of hearts that they did the best they could to prepare and perform in any undertaking. These kinds of values and characteristics are timeless and relevant in many different spheres of life, not just in the classroom or on the court. We are all in the game of endurance—"enduring to the end"— and that is why I believe these qualities are so important to be taught to our children. It's not about the trophy on the shelf or the blue ribbons, it's about teaching and helping our children reach their true potential and ultimately become the best THEY can be.

NOTES

1. Tom Brady, interview by Matthew McConaughey, "New Again: Tom Brady," Interview, accessed March 10, 2015, http://www.interviewmagazine.com/culture/new-again-tom-brady/print/.

2. Allen Fox, *Tennis: Winning the Mental Match* (Kearney, NE: Morris Publishing, 2010), 14.

3. Ibid., 17–18.

4. Billie Jean King, *Pressure is a Privilege: Lessons I've Learned from Life and the Battle of the Sexes* (New York: Life Media, Inc., 2008), 107.

5. Theodore Roosevelt, "The Man in the Arena," from *Citizenship in a Republic* (speech given at the Sorbonne, Paris, on April 23, 1910).

6. Michael Jordan, in Robert Goldman and Stephen Papson *Nike Culture: The Sign of the Swoosh* (London: Sage Publications, 1998), 49.

7. *Kung Fu Panda*, directed by John Stevenson and Mark Osborne (Hollywood, CA: Paramount Pictures, 2008).

LIFE LESSON #23

TURN TO A HIGHER POWER WHEN IN NEED

"I have been driven many times upon my knees by the overwhelming conviction that I had nowhere else to go. My own wisdom and that of all about me seemed insufficient for that day."[1]

—Attributed to Abraham Lincoln

In teaching our children to become the best THEY can be, teach them that in their hour of need, there will always be a higher power for them to turn to for comfort and support.

There have been many times in my life where I've been put in positions where I have felt that my natural capabilities were not sufficiently adequate to handle the enormity of the situation. One of these times was when I was warming up on an outside court at Wimbledon, getting ready to play in the quarterfinal round against the world's number one player, Ivan Lendl, on court two—the Graveyard Court. Because I had just beaten Mark Woodforde on that court in straight sets, I was feeling comfortable and confident about my chances of beating Ivan there.

It wasn't too big or overwhelming of a stadium, so it was really about the tennis that was played on the court rather than anything else, and I was playing very good tennis at that time. However, during my warm-up, a runner from the Head Referee's office came out to inform me that our match was now being put on Centre Court due to rain delays. This changed things dramatically. First of all, I had never played on Centre Court. Second, our match was now going to be broadcast on worldwide television. I was excited about the opportunity to be sure, but this turn of events immediately took me outside of my comfort zone.

As I was in the locker room getting ready for the match, I noticed Ivan getting a massage to get loosened up because it was just about time for us to be escorted out onto the court. It was now time for me to get loosened up, so I stepped into one of the bathroom stalls for privacy and got down on my knees and prayed. I didn't pray for victory but prayed for the strength to handle the situation well and to have the capacity to perform without fear to the best of my ability. While I didn't win the match, I believe my prayer was answered.

One of my favorite pieces of art is Arnold Friberg's "The Prayer at Valley Forge," which captures George Washington kneeling down in the snow in solemn prayer. It is a reminder that all of us need to spend more time on our knees praying for help and guidance.

NOTES

1. Abraham Lincoln to a friend, in Noah Brooks *Harper's Weekly*, July 1865.

ENJOY EACH STAGE OF LIFE

*"One of the most tragic things I know about human nature is that
all of us tend to put off living. We are all dreaming of some
magical rose garden over the horizon—instead of enjoying the roses
that are blooming outside our windows today."* [1]

—Dale Carnegie

Cindi and I fully took advantage of what the Tour lifestyle had to offer. When I wasn't practicing or playing matches, "Team Pearce" was out sightseeing and giving our young children the opportunity to experience the great cities—and their respective cultures—around the world. We thoroughly enjoyed this stage of our lives.

I passed this thought along to Ramsay Smith, son of tennis legend and Wimbledon champion Stan Smith, when I was coaching with the USTA in their national player development program prior to BYU. (Along with Ramsay, Andy Roddick, James Blake, and Mardy Fish were also a part of this group of players.) One day, after a training session in Florida, Ramsay asked me what I thought about him turning pro after high school or going to college. I told him that I thought he should enjoy each stage in life and go to college, and then see what happens from there. I wasn't his advisor, but he asked my opinion, and I gave it to him. (For the record, Ramsay ended up going to Duke and is now their head men's tennis coach, doing an incredible job developing and mentoring his players.)

The summer after his high school graduation, I bumped into Stan on the stairs going up to the players' lounge at Wimbledon. He pulled me aside, letting me know that he had a story he wanted to share with me. Stan explained that Ramsay was his high school's valedictorian and he used "enjoying each stage of life" as one of the themes of his graduation speech that he had learned from one of his "elders." I guess Stan learned about the conversation that Ramsay and I had and knew I was the elder that Ramsay referred to.

I first heard this expression used by the Covey children, hearing how their parents were always advising them to smell the roses, to not get caught up in "the thick of thin things" (as Dr. Covey would say), and to enjoy each stage of life, whether as a junior high or high school student, a collegiate athlete hoping for the pros, a "starving" student, a young married couple, a stay-at-home mother overwhelmed by her rambunctious children, or a middle-ager like me who has children spread from ages twenty-six to twelve—all in different stages of their lives. Having learned this from the Coveys, I now pass it on to your family. Teach your children to enjoy each stage of their lives—and pass it on!

NOTES

1. Dale Carnegie, *How to Stop Worrying and Start Living: Time-Tested Methods for Conquering Worry* (New York: Pocket Books, 1990).

LIFE LESSON #25

WHEREVER YOU ARE, THAT'S WHERE YOU ARE

"To a large degree, the measure of our peace of mind is determined by how much we are able to live in the present moment. Irrespective of what happened yesterday or last year, and what may or may not happen tomorrow, the present moment is where you are—always!"[1]

—Richard Carlson

One summer, I was playing a warm-up tournament to Wimbledon in Manchester, England. It had been raining for days on end (as it does from time to time in England) and no matches were able to be played. All of the players were holed up in the players' lounge at the facility from morning until night (because you had to be on-site in case there was a break in the weather). I remember thinking during those days of complete inactivity that I wished I was anywhere but there. Wow, how immature and spoiled I was! Sure, there were days like this, and some weeks and some cities around the world were better than others, but what a life it was; it's hard to beat the life of a tennis pro.

Midway through the week and not feeling happy with myself because of my poor attitude (it was likely that Cindi was not feeling happy with me because of my poor attitude), I resolved to change. Every morning when I left the hotel for the rest of that week in Manchester, and for the rest of that year and the next from city to city, I never went to a tennis site without a plentiful supply of books, magazines, newspapers, and so on. I had started into my independent study program at BYU, so I also had schoolwork with me to keep myself busy and active so I didn't get caught in the doldrums again.

In his book, *Don't Sweat the Small Stuff . . . And It's All Small Stuff*, author Richard Carlson put it this way: "As you focus more on becoming more peaceful with where you are, rather than focusing on where you would *rather* be, you begin to find peace right now, in the present. Then, as you move around, try new things, and meet new people, you carry that sense of inner peace with you."[2]

Since this experience in Manchester, and through the wisdom of Carlson, I really try to be where I am and get the most of the experience. Now, I hate to bring up Master Oogway again, but Carlson's reference to "inner peace" brings to mind one of my favorite scenes from *Kung Fu Panda* (my daughter Tara's favorite movie), when Shifu comes to him in a panic telling him that he has bad news. His classic response, "Ah, Shifu. There is just news. There is no good or bad."[3] Teach your children to get the most out of every situation they're in and that wherever they are, that's where they are.

NOTES

1. Richard Carlson, *Don't Sweat the Small Stuff . . . And It's All Small Stuff: Simple Ways to Keep the Little Things from Taking Over Your Life* (Paris: Hachette, 1996), 29.

2. Ibid., 134.

3. *Kung Fu Panda*, directed by John Stevenson and Mark Osborne (Hollywood, CA: Paramount Pictures, 2008).

LIFE LESSON #26

REDUCE FRICTION AND FRICTION POINTS

"A critic looking at these tightly focused, targeted interventions might dismiss them as Band-Aid solutions. But that phrase should not be considered a term of disparagement. The Band-Aid is an inexpensive, convenient, and remarkably versatile solution to an astonishing array of problems. In their history, Band-Aids have probably allowed millions of people to keep working or playing tennis or cooking or walking when they would otherwise have had to stop. The Band-Aid solution is actually the best kind of solution because it involves solving a problem with the minimum amount of effort and time and cost."[1]

—Malcolm Gladwell

One thing that Cindi and I have discussed more than a few times is how much easier things would have been traveling around the world back in the day with something we take for granted today: the ubiquitous cell phone and the Internet. A cell phone and the Internet would have gone a long way in reducing some "friction" in our lives back then. I don't mean friction terms of arguing, fighting, or anything like that. What I do mean, however, is looking for things in our lives that could be done more efficiently to get better results.

Let me give you an example. Before the 2010 tennis season at BYU, I was thinking about what I could do to operate my team in more efficient ways to become more successful. One thing that came to mind was how inefficient our travel habits had been. On road trips, after getting off a plane, retrieving all of our baggage, getting our rental cars, and heading toward our practice site, the guys would always be hungry. So we would have to stop and waste precious time trying to get ten guys through a sandwich shop and take the time to eat. This was time we could have been on the court practicing and getting adjusted to new conditions. So I made a policy that if anyone wanted to eat before practice on road trips they could bring a sandwich with them, buy one at the airport before departing, or starve—the choice didn't matter to me. We would now go straight from the airport to the practice site. And what a difference that made in our results beginning that season as we went undefeated in conference play to become Mountain West Conference Champions. The following year, we went undefeated again in conference play and beat TCU for the second time that season to also win the conference tournament.

There were other small things I instituted, along with this policy, but this was the one, I believe, that made the biggest difference. And it was simple. Reducing friction is a very broad term and can mean many different things. It can also mean to reduce friction points, those things that lead to confrontation, frustration, or anger—all inefficiencies.

After this cause-and-effect example with my team, Cindi and I then went about trying to reduce friction points in our home—and we're still at it today. As I learned through my team experience, reducing friction in even small ways can make a big difference in achieving better results.

NOTES

1. Malcolm Gladwell, *The Tipping Point: How Little Things Can Make a Big Difference* (New York: Back Bay Books, 2002).

TEACH YOUR CHILDREN TO MAKE THEIR LIVES A MISSION TO MAKE A DIFFERENCE

"Everyone has his own specific vocation or mission in life to carry out a concrete assignment which demands fulfillment. Therein he cannot be replaced, nor can his life be repeated. Thus, everyone's task is unique as his specific opportunity to implement it."[1]

—Viktor E. Frankl

My parents instilled in me from an early age the idea that my entire life could be a mission through tennis and that I could make a difference. As a Mormon tennis player on the Tour, I, along with Cindi and our children, had unique opportunities within the tennis world to show that we were devout in our faith, but that we were also normal people. Over a ten-year period of traveling and interacting with fellow players, tournament officials, and fans from all over the world, I believe we were able to accomplish this personal mission.

Shortly after my loss to Lendl, I was ushered in to a press conference with members of the media from all over the world. One question I was asked, because reaching the quarterfinals of a grand slam was my largest "purse" (prize money earned) to date, was what I was going to do with my paycheck. Jordan was our only child at the time, so my answer was that we wanted to have more children. The prize money I received from Wimbledon would certainly help toward that end. It got back to me that Arthur Ashe, whom I had met when he commentated at my Easter Bowl

Championship win as a junior in 1984, had attended this press conference and was floored by my answer, expecting a more typical answer like "buy a new sports car" or something more along those lines. This was one of the few times I publicly took the opportunity to share what motivated me. The most important thing, however, was the week-to-week "mission" of trying to be a great competitor and not be a jerk at the same time. This, in the end, would make more a difference than anything I might have to say in a public setting.

Cindi and I are grateful for the many friendships we have formed with people from all over the world through tennis. While they have made a difference in our lives, we also hope we've made a difference in theirs. Teach your children that their lives are missions and that, in their own unique way, as Frankl suggests, they too can and will make a difference.

NOTES

1.   Viktor E. Frankl, *Man's Search for Meaning* (Boston: Beacon Press, 2006).

LIFE LESSON #28

FINISH STRONG

"It's the final steps of a journey that create an arrival."[1]

—Sam Parker

Through the years, the phrase *finish strong* has become a constant theme on my teams at BYU because I use the expression a lot. Tennis is a lot like chess with a distinct opening, middle, and endgame. (While I'm a mediocre player at best, I love chess and am always trying to improve my game.) Like chess, you could play brilliant in the opening and middle, but if you blow it at the end, whatever you did before doesn't really matter. It has been argued by the pundits that tennis is one of the most—if not *the* most—difficult sports to play mentally because of the scoring system. Every game is a zero-sum game, as well as every set, and there's not a clock to run out if you get a big lead because of your brilliant play at the beginning or middle of a game or set. And you have to win the last point, like getting the last out in baseball, which can be difficult when the pressure is on.

My experience as a player trying to close out a set or a match, combined with eighteen years of coaching and twenty-six years of being a parent, has taught me that it's the endgame, like in chess, that is the most important in the classroom and on the court. When it gets down to the end of a match, or the end of a long semester and it's time for the final, it's at these times when we are most likely to succumb to the pressure and not finish as strong as when we started. Forewarned is forearmed. At these critical junctures in our children's lives, when they are in their "endgame" phase of whatever it is that they are doing, teach and remind them often to finish strong. While these are just two simple words, they carry a lot of meaning and can make a huge difference in their attitude, fortitude, commitment, and confidence to finish what they started on as high of note as possible. When I tell members of my team to finish strong, and when Cindi and I remind our children to finish strong, they know exactly what is meant.

NOTES

1. Sam Parker, *212: The Extra Degree* (Bedford, TX: Walk the Talk Company, 2005), 33.

CHOOSING A "DOUBLES" PARTNER

"Happy is the man who finds a true friend, and far happier is he who finds that true friend in his wife."

—Unknown

The best advice I've ever heard about choosing a doubles partner is actually very simple counsel: choose someone better than you. Fortunately, in the game of life, I did exactly that. I married someone much better than me, and my children and I have been greatly blessed because of it.

In the fall of 1986 after I had just turned pro, I went on my first trip to Asia with stops in Tokyo and Hong Kong. Having never been to these cities before, it was an exciting trip as a professional tennis player traveling on the ATP Tour. When I arrived in Hong Kong, I wasn't expecting this city to be as beautiful as it was. It's truly an incredible city: vibrant, abuzz with activity, and green and lush juxtaposed against one of the most modern skylines in the world. This city is truly a marvel.

One thing was missing, though, with my new, exciting life, visiting all of these great places, staying in the finest hotels, and getting paid to do something I loved. It was just too good to be true. Despite all of these great things, I was like the lone man in the Garden of Eden. I felt empty that I didn't have someone to share my life and these experiences with. When I proposed to Cindi a few months later, I was the happiest man on the planet at that moment in time when she said yes. She traveled with me, only missing trips on occasion, for the rest of my career. She is a great "doubles" partner; I'm fortunate to have found her.

One of my favorite stories about Cindi comes from Wimbledon in 1991. Cindi and another wife (Gina Arias) cofounded the ATP Tour Wives and Girlfriends Association earlier in the year, and Cindi became the first president. Their goal was to make Tour life better for wives, girlfriends (the WAGs, as they say), and families. They also wanted to perform charity work and have a vehicle to make it easier for them to form friendships with each other and have something to do while we (the guys) were doing our tennis thing. They were treated as a formidable, high-powered force on the Tour—which they were. Needless to say, there was a lot of buzz and interest about this newly formed association when Wimbledon rolled around in June.

A few days before Wimbledon started, the telephone in our flat rang, and I picked it up, expecting it to be a family member. (We didn't give out our number to anyone other than family, so that's who I was expecting to be on the line.) The person on the line asked if he was speaking with Brad Pearce. I answered yes. He then identified himself as a reporter for BBC radio and wanted to do a live on-air story. At this point, I was thinking I was a real big-shot, figuring that the London press wanted to hear about what I thought my chances were for Wimbledon success after reaching the quarters the previous year. Instead, he asked, "Is your wife, Cindi, there? I would like to have a word with her, if you don't mind?" She was the one they wanted to interview.

A day later, she was in the BBC studio giving an interview on national radio about their association. Not only was she a great WAG by giving me the support I needed, but she was also an incredible mother to our children on the road and loved the adventure. And she was a great president, working with tournament directors to make Tour life better, performing charity work, and creating an organization that allowed friendships to form with fellow wives and girlfriends. She said she modeled it after the Relief Society organization. She also gave a great interview on BBC radio that day. She was the superstar.

I said it at the beginning. The life lesson here—teach your children to find the right "doubles" partner: someone who is better than them. I'm grateful that I did. It's made all the difference.

GRATITUDE AND LEGACY

"To express gratitude is gracious and honorable,
to enact gratitude is generous and noble, but to live
with gratitude ever in our hearts is to touch heaven."[1]

—Thomas S. Monson

In this, my last life lesson, I want to share one of the most important things that I've learned on my road to Wimbledon and since—and that's gratitude. It would have been impossible for me to accomplish what I did in tennis without a whole host of people teaching, helping, coaching, and guiding me every step of the way, beginning with my parents and siblings. I'm grateful for my coaches through the years, Cindi and her parents, and friends and mentors that have made an impact on my life.

One of my favorite poems sums up how I feel as I bring this book to a close. It's by the English poet John Donne:

> *No man is an island entire of itself; every man*
> *is a piece of the continent, a part of the main;*
> *if a clod be washed away by the sea, Europe*
> *is the less, as well as if a promontory were, as*
> *well as any manner of thy friends or of thine*
> *own were; any man's death diminishes me,*
> *because I am involved in mankind.*
> *And therefore never send to know for whom*
> *the bell tolls; it tolls for thee.*[2]

Each of us matters; we are all "part of the main." My family has family themes that we put up on our walls, which we introduce at the beginning of each year. We started this in 2002. I don't remember where we got the idea from. My guess is that saw it in another home, or read about in the *Ensign* or some other family magazine. We have been the recipients of many "pass-alongs" through the years for which we are most grateful. That is how we all learn from each other for the betterment of ourselves and our children. One of them was this message from Latter-day Saint President Gordon B. Hinckley:

> You have nothing in this world more precious than your children. When you grow old, when your hair turns white and your body grows weary, when you are prone to sit in a rocker and meditate on the things of your life, nothing will be so important as the question of how your children have turned out. It will not be the money you have made. It will not be the cars you have owned. It will not be the large house in which you live. The searing question that will cross your mind again and again will be, *How well have my children done?*[3]

It is my sincere hope and desire that some thought, concept, or idea in these Life Lessons will help you to teach, guide, and train your children to become the best THEY can be. If there was, I hope you will use it and pass it on. I will be grateful. That is how we all learn from each other for the betterment of ourselves and our children. That is how we all become the best we can be.

NOTES

1. Thomas S. Monson, "President Monson: Divine Gift of Gratitude," accessed March 12, 2015, https://www.lds.org/prophets-and-apostles/unto-all-the-world/monson-divine-gift-of-gratitude?lang=eng.

2. John Donne, "Meditation XVII" *Devotions Upon Emergent Occasions, and Severall Steps in My Sicknes*, in Dalhousie University, https://web.cs.dal.ca/~johnston/poetry/island.html.

3. Gordon B. Hinckley, "Your Greatest Challenge, Mother," October 2000, https://www.lds.org/general-conference/2000/10/your-greatest-challenge-mother?lang=eng.

APPENDIX

Left: Trying my Rod Laver grip as a four-year-old.

Below: Galea Cup, Belgrade, former Yugoslavia, 1985.

Right top: Junior Wimbledon, 1984.

Right middle: NCAA Championships, 1986.

Right bottom: French Open, May 1994.

UCLA practice with Coach Glenn Bassett and Assistant Coach Ron Cornell.

With Ronald and Nancy Reagan, 1990.

With Senator Orrin Hatch, 1990.

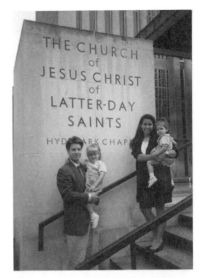

Top left: Jordan and Tara pretending to be ball kids at Wimbledon, 1993.

Top right: Going to church in London, 1993.

Bottom: Wimbledon, June 1994.

Above: Dubai Open, 1995.

Left: ATP Tour Trading Card.

ABOUT THE AUTHOR

B rad Pearce is now in his twelfth year as head coach for men's tennis at Brigham Young University. Born and raised in Provo, Utah, and later referred to by tennis icon Bud Collins as the "Provo Powerhouse" and "Stormin' Mormon," he graduated from Timpview High School in 1984. That same year, he reached the number one ranking in the United States as a junior tennis player and number five in the world. After high school, he attended UCLA, where he was a two-time all-American before turning pro after his sophomore year. As a professional he had ten career titles and wins over many legends of the sport, including a quarterfinal appearance on Centre Court at Wimbledon—making him one of thirty-seven Americans to reach the final eight at Wimbledon since the Open era of tennis. He has been inducted into the Utah Tennis Hall of Fame, Utah Sports Hall of Fame, and ITA Collegiate Tennis Hall of Fame. He was voted MWC Coach of the Year, ITA Mountain Region Coach of the Year twice, was the recipient of the USTA's National Campus and Community Outreach award, and was recognized as the Professional Tennis Registry's Jim Verdieck National Collegiate Coach of the Year. Despite his achievements through the years as a player and coach, his greatest satisfaction has come from teaming with his wife, Cindi, in raising their six children.